Dear Brian & Judy,

One can never receive too much love, friendship or books about roses!

Love,

Ken & Wen

A Heritage of ROSES

A Heritage of

HAZEL LE ROUGETEL

ROSES

Stemmer House

PUBLISHERS, INC.

OWINGS MILLS, MARYLAND

Dedicated to lovers of roses the world over

Inquiries should be directed to
STEMMER HOUSE PUBLISHERS, INC
2627 Caves Road
Owings Mills, Maryland, 21117

Printed and bound in Italy by New Interlitho S.P.A.

A Barbara Holdridge book
First U.S. Edition

Designed by Norman Reynolds
Drawings by Diana Mead

ISBN 0–88045–110–6

Contents

Acknowledgments

While writing this book, I have endeavoured to express in the appropriate context my appreciation of help from many kind people at home and abroad. If I have omitted any along the way, I hope they will forgive me and be assured that I am truly grateful for any gesture, however small, which has made a contribution to my story. To all the libraries I have used worldwide, particularly The Royal Horticultural Society's Lindley Library in London, I owe a great deal. To Graham Thomas for his generous consideration, to members of the Garden History Society for ready replies to queries in their own spheres of expertise, to my family and friends for their patience and encouragement – specially my daughter, Heather Angel, for her expert scrutiny of my photographs – to all I would like to say thank you for the part played in this production.

The Author and publishers would like to thank the following for the use of their photographs and illustrations on the pages listed.

The RHS Lindley library for illustrations and photographs from *Figures of Plants* by Miller, 12; The Reeve's Collection, 38; *Journal of Horticulture* (1888), 68; *Gardeners' Magazine* (1908), 100; *Gardeners' Chronicle* (1908), 112; *The Garden*, (1873) 129. The Fawcett Library, City of London Polytechnic, for illustrations taken from *The Queen*, (1897–1914) 99, 101, 104, 108. Robert Le Rougetel, 117, 170. The Hunt Institute for Botanical Documentation (Pittsburgh) for the extract from Walahfrid Strabo's *Hortulus*, 9.

Foreword

by Graham Stuart Thomas

THE Rose is a much travelled flower. It has followed civilizations in their peregrinations across the world. Authors have been inspired to write books about the genus for almost 200 years – botanical treatises, details of cultivation and volumes of beauty. Occasionally a book has been written which unites the outlook of mankind to the appraisal of roses. Hazel Le Rougetel has contributed to these rarities.

There is no doubt that the Rose was first treasured for its fragrance, long before plants were fully assessed and regardless of beauty. The lasting scent of the dried petals of roses was unique, but the distillation of rose-water from the flowers was a great discovery: this was a commodity which, in its day, was the supposed antidote for innumerable ills. The much more precious Attar, an oil floating on the surface of rose-water, was worth more than its weight in gold. This oily substance is used to flavour the pink portions of marshmallows and Turkish Delight and I have noticed of late years that it is becoming more popular as a perfume for ladies. Small wonder, perhaps, considering the esteem in which it has been held since its discovery in India in the sixteenth century. Roses were first prized, for their fragrance and secondly for their beauty; to those qualities as the centuries pass, their garden value has been added, since gardens were steered away from mere produce to enjoyment.

In this way, wherever they grow, roses have been taken to heart by gardeners. In addition there is the fact that some 150 species with five petals only grow wild around the Northern Hemisphere. Of these only a mere handful have become the darlings of horticulture; favouritism has been due almost entirely to hybrids which cropped up long before history was written or records were remembered, resulting in double flowers with more staying power and even more scent. To prehistoric hybrids in Europe and the Middle East were added a group of hybrids of equally ancient origin from China, at the close of the eighteenth century.

The resulting confluence has been like the uniting of two great rivers, determined by the flow of civilization crossing from east to west and back again and from north to south with reverse traffic likewise. The shapes of flowers, their recurrence, their colours and scents have all played their part in competing for favour in the eyes of gardeners the world over. In this way roses have gathered unto themselves more love and history, lore and legend than any other genus. Few who grow roses today can be oblivious of this fact, but if any there be, the pages of this book will dispel their ignorance.

Hazel Le Rougetel was brought up in the country and from early days was enthralled by gardening. After a busy early life she found at last that she had the time to return to and develop this former love, some twenty-five years ago. It was then that our paths crossed, at Sunningdale Nurseries, where my collection of old French roses was established. I have watched her growing interest, enthusiasm and knowledge of roses develop. She fortunately has had time of late years to dig and delve into rose history. This has been done not only by lengthy research in libraries – including her own – but also by meeting rose growers in many countries. Knowing how time-consuming work in libraries can be, I am able to guess at the weeks and months of study that has gone into her preparatory work. But that is nothing to the time and energy needed to travel some 100,000 miles to distant countries to see for herself numerous rose gardens and to meet fellow enthusiasts. For many years she has been receiving – and giving in exchange – views and news, anecdotes and points of history which had nearly been forgotten.

These experiences have been welded into an absorbing story which will hold the attention by its combination of deep research and clarity of image, coupled with delight. Though it is so personal an account, the book has undoubtedly an international value concerning roses old and new and their place in various nations' hearts. Hazel shares generously with us all the knowledge she has so devotedly gathered, in both history and theory, and also in a practical garden way, with aesthetics never neglected. Her concluding chapters reveal this and prove that her desire in making this record is to encourage us all to create beautiful gardens. Only a skilled practitioner could do this in the form of a story – a truthful one, about a genus which has attracted more authors than any other – the genus Rosa.

Part I

FIRST ROSES IN ENGLAND AND AMERICA

No man can say
No man remember, how many uses there are
For Oil of Roses as a cure for mankind's ailments.

WALAHFRID STRABO, *Hortulus*, 1510

R. gallica officinalis

CHAPTER 1

Old Summer Flowerers

ROSES of the past have become roses of
the present. I wonder, though, how much thought goes with their purchase
and planting. I am sure some is given to choice of colour and placing in the
garden, but suspect that few questions arise in the mind as to how these
selected roses evolved or where they came from originally. I believe that a little
knowledge of their history and of those who contributed to their development
must enhance their value for many growers today.

When I take visitors around my small garden, as well as demonstrating how
variety of habit may best be utilized and diverse charms displayed, I am also
able to illustrate a chronological story of roses. This usually leads to eager
questioning and resolve to learn more. Perhaps what follows may help to take
others further back along a path bordered by the first few grown in gardens, to

follow it round three centuries and to discover how they increased to the present abundance of beauty.

Wild roses, collected from the countryside, were used to embellish arbours and fencing in medieval times and, with them 'Roses red and white' often appear in pictures and descriptions of early gardens. These were Gallica and Alba, to be followed by Damask, Centifolia and Moss; at high summer filling gardens with a delicious fragrance from shapely blooms of soft shades. To a quiet accompaniment from busy bees and gentle fountains, gardeners of the seventeenth century would wander among their roses and herbs, content, with no concept of the great change to come.

The original single Gallica, *R. rubra*, one of the hardiest of roses, originated in southern Europe and a notable descendant, *R. gallica officinalis*, semi-double, bright cerise pink with prominent yellow stamens, was described by ancient writers throughout Europe and the Middle East. An early evocative reference comes from the *Hortulus* of Walahfrid Strabo, a German monk writing of garden flowers in the ninth century, although his charming work was not published in Vienna until six centuries later. From the thirteenth century this rose was grown extensively in Provins, south-east of Paris, and was much valued for its sweet-scented flowers, which were used in the preparation of conserves, perfumes and medicines. The English herbalist, Culpeper, rated it highly for treatment of disorders of the head, eyes, gums, heart and stomach (*The English Physitian Enlarged*, 1652) and thus it became generally known as 'The Apothecary's Rose'. According to Thomas Rivers, a Victorian rosarian, this rose was widely grown in Surrey for use by London druggists and he also quoted, in his *The Rose Amateur's Guide* (1837–77), a French source on its historic association:

> Somewhere about the year 1277 the son of the King of England [Edmund Earl of Lancaster], who had taken the title of Comte of Champagne, was sent by the King of France to Provins with troops to avenge the murder of the mayor of that city . . . on his return to England he took for his device the red rose of Provins . . .
>
> (Opoix, *L'Ancien Provins*)

This was later to become the emblem of the House of Lancaster.

An early sport of this rose named 'Rosa Mundi' has dramatic blooms striped pink and crimson, one often reverting entirely to the 'Apothecary' pink. This was recorded by Sir Thomas Hanmer in his *Garden Book* of 1659 as being 'first found in Norfolk a few years since upon a branch of the common Red Rose and from thence multiplied'. 'Tuscany' is another beautiful ancient Gallica, once known as 'Old Velvet' on account of crimson-maroon shades shimmering as the sheen on sumptuous cloth.

The white rose of early gardens was believed to be *R. × alba*, a natural hybrid of *R. damascena* and *R. canina*. This was also grown in Greek and Roman gardens and is considered the most classic form of the rose, often depicted in Renaissance paintings. *R. × alba* 'Semi-plena', semi-double with golden stamens, was taken by Edward IV (1461–70) as his personal badge and thus became the White Rose of York. *R. × alba* 'Maxima', a full-petalled white, gained the name 'The Jacobite Rose' from the legend that it had been

'Rosa Mundi' recorded as a sport of 'The
Apothecary's Rose' in the sixteenth century.

Plate CCXXI of Philip Miller's *Figures of Plants* (1755–60), with relatively recent 'Moss Provence', left and older variegated Damask 'York and Lancaster'.

placed in the bonnet of Bonnie Prince Charlie by Flora Macdonald and was thus cherished by his followers. A pre-fifteenth-century variety, known in Britain as 'Great Maiden's Blush' and in France as 'Cuisse de Nymph' is appropriately named for its delicate pink shading and pure fragrance.

R. damascena, renowned for wonderful perfume and grown in Persia and eastern Mediterranean countries before the time of the Crusades, was collected and distributed throughout Europe, particularly in Bulgaria, where a great industry for distilling attar of roses was established. Virgil wrote of roses flowering twice yearly and undoubtedly these would have been the ancient *R. damascena semperflorens*, believed to have been grown in Pompeii. Sir Thomas Hanmer described this as 'a very Damask in leaves and flower and scent, but it bears two or three moneths more than the ordinary damask and very plentifully if it stand warm'. Double pink flowers are loosely formed and it is now known as 'The Autumn Damask' or 'Quatre Saisons'. A bi-coloured Damask, *R. damascena versicolor*, is sometimes confused with 'Rosa Mundi' (*R. gallica* 'Versicolor'), but the former is blotched pink and white, never striped with crimson and sometimes blooms entirely of each shade are borne on the same bush. Largely due to an account by Shakespeare in *King Henry VI*, Part I, Act II, Scene 4 this Damask has become known as 'York and Lancaster'. The red and white roses of Lancaster and York were united to form the symbolic Tudor Rose when Henry VII married his cousin, Elizabeth of York.

Two examples of recreated historic gardens with roses can be found in Hampshire today. Queen Eleanor's Garden, off Winchester Great Hall, named for the queens of Henry I and Edward I – from Provence and Castile respectively – has been designed by Drs John Harvey and Sylvia Landsberg with entire authenticity and much sensitivity. Here 'roses red and white' of the thirteenth century adorn a trellised turf seat and, intertwined with honeysuckle and vine, will soon cover a tunnel arbour. More elaborate garden diversions become evident in the Tudor House Garden, Southampton, also designed by Sylvia Landsberg, where a dozen different roses now embellish a close walk and arbour surrounding an immaculate knot garden of greys and greens, borders bright with cornflower and marigold, a fountain set in camomile lawn and a tiny secret corner, to be viewed through a bay hedge peephole, for raised bee skeps, thatch-protected and embellished by *R. gallica officinalis* at midsummer.

Towards the end of the sixteenth century another rose was developed by the Dutch from strains of existing garden varieties. The full-petalled Centifolia or 'Cabbage Rose' is often seen in still-life paintings of the time and ever since is thus called Rose des Peintres. With strong scent and bold bloom, these roses of Provence, as they became known, were the type to be offered 'in greatest plenty' by eighteenth-century nurserymen. The fifth class of old summer-flowering roses evolved as a Centifolia sport (*R. × centifolia muscosa*) with mossiness on bud and flower stalk formed by a glandular, bristly growth with a rather astringent scent. It first occurred in 1696 and, being a novelty, was sought with eagerness by curious gardeners of the day. Mosses maintained a place in Victorian gardens, but it was not until the middle of this century that an interest was revived in all types of old roses.

In general, they are hardy, comparatively healthy and of wonderful colour and fragrance, but varying form of habit must be taken into account when planning to grow them today. Although further detailed advice on their care and how best to display them will be found in Part VI, a general description as an aid to identification and mention of a few rewarding examples is relevant here. Gallicas make rather formal, compact bushes, rarely more than 4 ft (1·2 m) high. Their flowers are mostly neat, borne on upright stems with many bristles; they provide a wonderful range of pink colouring from palest to darkest tint and the rough leaves are usually a clear green. Deep 'Charles de Mills' is one of the most perfect in form (I think it must be very like a rose referred to in the eighteenth century by Philip Miller as appearing to be 'clipped with scissars') and 'Président de Sèze' is an example of a shaded Gallica, deep pink and lilac, paling towards the petal edges.

In contrast, more robust upstanding bushes of Albas have glaucous foliage, dependably disease-resistant, making a good foil for their white or pale pink blooms borne on green stems with thorns and curved prickles. They adapt well to most situations, even to growing tall on a north wall. Pale pinks 'Céleste', with perfect scrolled buds and 'Félicité Parmentier', developing from unusual yellowish ones, are among the most beautiful in this group. Damasks provide a more informal display, many with lax, open bushes, their white or pink blooms on stems armed with bristles and prickles and some inclining their heads amidst soft green downy foliage, like 'Madame Hardy', white with a green eye and very much esteemed, although 'Leda' or 'Painted Damask' is of more compact growth and better deportment with pale blooms, tipped crimson.

Centifolias are the most substantial of these old roses: bushes are robust, stems well-armed, foliage – dull green compared with the others – is rather coarse and drooping and flowers are extremely full, tending to fall with weight. Some do not make elegant growth and are better disciplined to contain recalcitrant habits. For instance, pale pink 'Fantin-Latour' has reached 8 ft (2·4 m) in my garden and needs strong support, but 'Robert de Diable', shaded crimson, remains about half the size. Mosses have the same characteristics although, of course, their mossiness provides immediate identification. Among

Queen Eleanor's Garden, beside Winchester's Great Hall, typical of the thirteenth century, with 'Roses Red and White'.

many later varieties, tall 'William Lobb', deep purple fading lilac, is magnificent, but far and away my favourite is the old 'Common Moss' of medium size, clear pink and most beautifully scented.

An early collector of roses abroad was John Tradescant the Elder (*c.* 1570–1638), gardener to the first Earl of Salisbury at his recently acquired Hatfield House in 1610. In the autumn of that year Tradescant was sent to the Low Countries and purchased roses in Leiden and Haarlem, including sixteen 'Province' (Centifolia). On his return he was busy remaking the garden at Salisbury House in the Strand and the purchase of many Sweet Briar and poles seems to indicate the construction of an arbour. Some came from Thomas Chandler, but for other roses, including 200 white standards, Tradescant went to France.

At Hatfield House some roses were grown among the soft fruit and included cuttings sent by Sir Henry Wootton, Ambassador in Venice. A catalogue of plants in the Tradescants' own Lambeth garden (1634) listed twenty-seven roses, and a second included in the records of their *Museum Tradescantianum* (1656) contained a further three. *R. muscovita* appears in both and was collected during an expedition to Archangel in 1618; 'of marvellous sweete scent' and likened to *R. cinnamomea* (now *R. majalis*). Both lists included *R. virginiana*, first grown in England by the Tradescants, although not collected by the Younger during his travels in Virginia.

In the churchyard of St Mary Lambeth today, the Marchioness of Salisbury has created a knot garden with plants of the Tradescants' time near their graves. Here, in the sheltered urban environment, the roses tend to flower a little earlier than in an open situation and are usually making a good display before midsummer. In the church itself, the Tradescant Trust has established a rewarding museum of garden history. A little further up-river, Chelsea Physic Garden was established for the Apothecaries of London in 1673; Philip Miller was in charge here for almost fifty years of the eighteenth century. In 1727 he was in Holland collecting plants and reported that his first sight of a Moss Rose was in the garden of Dr Boerhaave (Professor of Medicine and Botany at the University of Leiden) 'who was so good as to give me one of the plants'. This he named 'Moss-Provence' and the distinctive bud was illustrated three years later in the *Catalogus Plantarum* of a 'Society of Gardeners' in London of which Miller was a member.

He also selected this rose for Plate CCXXI in his *Figures of Plants* (1755–60), a work which illustrated some of those plants described in *The Gardeners Dictionary*. The latter, recognized as the most important work on eighteenth-century gardening, reached eight editions in the author's lifetime; in the first, 1731, forty-six roses were listed. In later editions these were split into twenty-two species roses and twenty-four described as 'the greatest variety of double roses now cultivated in English gardens'. As well as in the flower garden, Miller advocated informal use of roses in the wilderness, 'the principal ornament of a fine garden', and suggested they be placed near walks where the scent would be appreciated. He would put low Scotch Briars in front of Gallicas, with taller Damask, Provence and Frankfurt behind, all to be associated with shrubs of like size and suitable underplanting below.

As the *Dictionary* was in the libraries of most landowners, advice on rose planting would have been carefully followed. In 1750 John Macclary, head

Illustration from *The Ladies Magazine*, 1826, when it was still fashionable to wear a full-blown Provence Rose in the hair.

gardener at Rousham, wrote to the absent owner (General Dormer, for whom William Kent had designed the garden) describing a walk to see 'deferant sorts of Flowers peeping through the deferant sorts of Evergreens, here you think the Laurel produces a Rose, the Holly, a Syringa, the Yew a Lilac . . .' Surprise was a frequent objective and, early in the 1740s, across the Border, Sir John Clerk of Penicuik contrived a most entertaining diversion in his extensive grounds where a river meandered below steep hills. Guests would be taken through Hurleycove, a dark, mysterious, stone-lined tunnel, allowed to pause in a subterranean chamber before continuing to the exit on the other side of the hill to find Hurley Ponds below a 'circular brae'. This, described by the owner was 'planted with oaks, firs, walnuts, ashes, plums, elms of all kinds and other sorts of Trees. The border of this circular ground near the walk is planted with sweet Bryer, Laurel, Rose bushes and a great variety of shrubs and flowers.' Here, after limbo, was unexpected paradise.

Roses were extensively used by 'Capability' Brown in his wild garden designs: 'Sweet Briar', Scots Briars, *R. foetida*, *R. cinnamomea*, 'Maiden's Blush' and 'Moss-Provence' were included in a 1748 list for Sir James Dashwood's pleasure grounds at Kirtlington Park. Between 1755 and 1757, of the 270 roses ordered in great variety, 140 were 'Sweet Briar': probably to be used for hedging in the extensive wilderness designed by Brown at Petworth in Sussex. He created a delightful small one for Sir Robert Drummond at Cadland in Hampshire, its perimeter path leading through woodland and emerging to provide vistas of the Isle of Wight across the Solent. Mr and Mrs Maldwin Drummond have recently restored this most faithfully from the Brown plan and it was gratifying to be able to suggest to them roses that Miller would have thought appropriate.

Another enthusiastic gardener, Gilbert White of Selborne, often referred to his sixth edition (1752) of the *Dictionary* in his own *Garden Kalendar* (1751–71). The 'Moss-Provence' was obviously a favourite at his home, The Wakes; one arrived from brother Tom in London in 1756 and five more were planted two years later. From these, White propagated many by layering (the method preferred by Miller) and found that small twigs struck more readily than large shoots. His roses represented the average gardener's collection of the time: 'Austrian Briar', 'York and Lancaster', 'Marbl'd Rose', 'Black Belgic' (probably a dark Gallica), 'Provence', 'Double-flowering Sweet Briar' (possibly 'Manning's Blush'), 'Musk' and one he called 'Monthly', ('Autumn Damask'). Today there is a fine collection of old roses at The Wakes (some subsequent to White's time), at their best around the beginning of July.

Peter Collinson, a friend of Miller, sent a copy of *The Gardeners Dictionary* to Pennsylvanian botanist John Bartram, in 1737. Perhaps the roses described led to requests because two years later Bartram wrote, 'The rose thee sent me proves to be ye common single rose and that thee sent me for ye double blossomed sweet briar is our common single sort. We have plenty of ye damask, provence, white, cinnamon and double red roses, but I never saw ye yellow rose yet'. Although Miller was one of the recipients of Bartram's collected seeds and plants, distributed in England by Peter Collinson, they did not correspond directly until 1755. In February 1756 'a few plants of our best sorts of Roses' were sent from Chelsea to Bartram at Kingsessing, near Philadelphia; the following year Bartram acknowledged a further consignment, while a list from him to Miller included 'highland roses and swamp roses'. The latter, *R. palustris*, is a moisture-loving counterpart of *R. carolina*, found in swampy areas from Lower Quebec to Florida.

Roses from America began to appear in English trade lists from the middle of the eighteenth century. In 1760 the nurseryman Hanbury of Church Langton, Leicestershire, a specialist in American plants, offered a 'Wild Virginian' and a 'Pennsylvanian' rose. Four years later John Whittingham at the Charter-house, near Coventry, advertised the 'Purple Cluster' from America at 1s, with 'American Sweet Brier' and 'Virgin or Thornless', both at 6d. The only item costing more than 1s in the list of forty-four roses was the 'Moss-Provence' at 2s. During the late 1780s, Barnes and Callender at the Orange-Tree, Briggate, Leeds, printed a list of fifty-six and included the 'Virgin' at 4d, a single 'Pennsylvanian' at 6d and a 'Double Pennsylvania' at 2s 6d, a price only exceeded by four European specialities: 'Demieux' ('De Meaux'), 'Tall Burgundy', 'Dwarf Burgundy', and 'Scarlet Sweet Brier'. Here I must acknowledge John Harvey's helpful expertise and for more detailed information concerning eighteenth-century rose prices, his articles in *The Rose Annual* for 1976 and 1979 should be consulted.

CHAPTER 2

Roses for Early American Gardens

In 1633 John Winthrop, Governor of Massachusetts, received a letter from his friend, Joseph Downing in London: 'If you have no roses there, in New England, I will send you over some damaske, red and white and Province rose plants, all of these three or four apiece, or more if need be.' If these were received, they would have been given a place in the kitchen garden. John Winthrop appreciated the culinary importance of roses: he advised his son to make sure that members of the family, shortly to leave England, be well supplied with 'a conserve of redd roses for the voyage'.

Records of William Penn's garden bear out this association of roses with fruit and vegetables; in 1686 his steward reported, 'Rasberries, Gooseberries, Currans, Quinces, Roses, Walnuts and Figs grow well', while Penn himself observed, 'Our Gardens supply us with all sorts of herbs and even some which are not in England. Here are roses, currants, gooseberries, turnips . . .'. The present Horticulturist at Pennsbury Manor, Charles S. Thomforde, has found nothing to confirm the story that William Penn brought out eighteen roses on his second trip from England to America. However, a book of medical and culinary recipes collected by Penn's mother-in-law and his first wife, Giuliema, was in use there by 1702, and a recipe containing rosewater was for 'ye palsie and ye giddiness of head'. In the *Journal* (1677–94) of Captain Laurence

'White Provence' or 'Unique Blanche', discovered in
Suffolk, 1775, treasured in new gardens far away for
delicate, silky petals.

'Sweet Briar' (*R. eglanteria*), long grown in gardens
for fragrance, was widely used by settlers in America
as protective hedges and screens.

Hammond of Charleston under 'Physical receipts', two quarts of 'Rosewater red' were needed as an ingredient for a 'Medicine to recover ye colour and complixion when lost by sickness'. This product was still of importance in 1790, when George Washington wrote to his gardener at Mount Vernon: 'Mrs Washington desires you will direct old Doll to distill a good deal of Rose and Mint Water.'

From visits to Massachusetts in 1638 and 1664, John Josselyn compiled a herbal and account of the natural history, both indigenous and imported, and mentioned roses in *New England Rarities Discovered* (1672). On *R. carolina* (of which there are many forms native to eastern and central North America) he said, 'Wild Damask Rose, single, but very large and sweet'. He appreciated English roses growing 'very pleasantly' and specifically mentioned the 'Sweet Bryer or Eglantine'. For practical purposes this rose was extensively used in new settlements as boundary hedging and to enclose gardens for a number of reasons. It grew very rapidly, lived long, was easily propagated from an abundance of seedlings and proved aesthetically pleasing with its fragrant foliage, all the stronger when freshly clipped. Thos. Ashe must have encountered it when compiling his *Observations* of 1682 on South Carolina: 'The gardens begin to be beautiful and adorned with herbs and flowers which to the smell or eye are pleasing and agreeable, viz. the Rose, Tulip, Carnation and Lilly, etc.'

'I set Sweet Briar Seeds at the Pasture of Sandersons next the lawn at the upper end' was an October 1686 diary note of Judge Samuel Sewell of Boston, and three years later William Penn sent instructions to John Blackwell at Pennsbury: 'Plow no more land than serves the house. Let the Gardiner when come take special care of getting quick setts and good speedy and quick shades ... let him plant wt. grows quickest, be sure woodbine and sweet brier, etc.'

By the turn of the century some houses in Philadelphia were developing more decorative gardens, as seen from a contemporary account of one in South Second Street, where Penn was staying in 1701: 'Edward Skippen has an orchard and garden adjoining to his big house that equalises any that I have seen, having a v. famous and pleasant summer house in the middle of his garden, abounding with tulips, pinks, carnations, roses (of various sorts), lilies, not to mention them that grow wild in our fields.' Some fifty years later, Sir Peter Warren of the Royal Navy had established an extensive garden in Greenwich Village, New York, said to be a 'veritable fairyland of Flowers' and in June appearing 'literally pink with roses'.

More detailed information on varieties of roses being grown in large gardens can be gleaned from a letter written by William Hamilton (London, 1785) to his private secretary at The Woodlands, near Philadelphia, where one of the most outstanding gardens in America was being created. Apparently he is answering a letter informing him of alarming plant losses and he asks,

Am I to infer that all the plants included under those numbers are dead – pray are none of the eastern plane, the portugal laurels (between 500 and 600), the evergreen sweet Briar, Singletons Rose, the evergreen Rose, the moscheute double rose, the white Damask rose, the variegated Damask rose, the yellow Austrian Rose, the Burgundy rose, the monthly Portland rose, the monthly red rose and the monthly variegated rose – now living?

He ends his letter with a query about a boundary hedge: 'You never mentioned what had been done to the ground on the west side of the road to Mrs George's or whether any Body had taken it to remove the Briars – I hope at any rate none of the suckers have been touched.'

The garden of John Cotton Smith in Sharon, Connecticut, seems to have been in the hands of his capable wife who kept a detailed diary at the end of the eighteenth century, recording, for instance, how she supervised the making of an asparagus bed and spent some time concocting rosewater from a collection of plants of which she was very proud. One rose received special mention: floriferous, double white, scented, it was treasured more than any other flower in the garden. This could have been the 'White Provence' or 'Unique Blanche', discovered in eastern England in 1775 and judged today by Peter Beales as one of the most beautiful of all white roses. There were ten others, perhaps purchased from the Prince nursery at Flushing, Long Island, whose first catalogue (1790) contained exactly that number of garden roses. The nursery had been established in 1737 by Robert Prince – 'the first American amateur to form an extensive collection of roses by making importations', wrote his grandson, William, in his *Manual of Roses* (New York, 1846). Other nurseries were offering more, for instance, John Lithen of Central Square, Philadelphia in 1783, but his list of eighteen contained many species.

Another rose enthusiast was a Boston merchant, Kirk Boott, who made an outstanding garden there around 1800. His son, a London doctor, recalled how his father would be up by 4 a.m. to tend his frames. Some seeds were obtained from Miniers in the Strand, then one of London's most reliable suppliers and patronized by many English landowners. Nurserymen had shops in this area too, as it was conveniently close to Covent Garden flower, fruit and vegetable market. Perhaps the young Dr Boott had been commissioned to seek out special roses for dispatch to Boston, as there was a certain enthusiasm for them in his family. Grown in the greenhouse to flower in December, they were taken indoors to brighten winter months and in the summer more than a hundred were blooming outside. These included the miniatures, 'Pompon' and 'De Meaux', Scots Briars, 'White Musk' and many summer flowerers.

Advertisements for roses from Europe had been appearing for some time in local papers. In the *Maryland Journal* of 21 January 1786, Peter Bellet was claiming to be the first French nurseryman and seedsman to offer plants and seeds direct to the public. Twenty-five varieties of monthly rose trees were included. In the same year the *South Carolina Gazette* announced an assortment of roses and bulbs from Holland and this paper also published a notice from John Chalvin & Co., 'Florists and Gardeners from France', stating that they had for sale many rose bushes of different colours.

Thomas Jefferson represents presidential appreciation of roses: they were used with geranium to decorate a window recess where he relaxed to listen to his favourite mocking bird when in town. In the country, as the practical gardener revealed through his *Garden Book* (1766–1824) (Reprinted Philadelphia, 1985), he made effective use of them around Monticello, his hill-top mansion overlooking Charlottesville in Virginia. He was planning his garden before the house was complete; seedlings of 'Sweet Briar' were planted in 1767, most likely to be used four years later in creating a shrubbery in open ground to the west, when he mentioned them with other roses, trees, climbing

Illustration from T. B. Jenkins, *Roses and Rose Culture* (New York 1892) showing 'Queen of the Prairies', eminently suitable for porch or verandah.

'Stanwell Perpetual',
from Lee of
Hammersmith, 1838,
soon recommended for
'exquisite fragrance' in
Pennsylvania by Robert
Buist

shrubby plants and hardy perennials. By 1782 Jefferson was keeping a calendar of his blooming plants, recording a crimson dwarf rose in flower from 20 May to 25 July and noting that it was a species.

In July 1791 he wrote to William Prince in Philadelphia to confirm an order made when he had visited the nursery the previous month. This was for three of each of ten varieties and conforms with the nursery's list issued the year before, with the exception of *R. cinnamomea*, substituted for the 'Red Damask' listed, possibly already growing at Monticello. Only two of each were received. Roses were among 'objects for the garden this year' (1794) and between 1808 and 1811 the *Garden Book* has a number of planting entries: some in the Poplar Forest, large roses of different kinds in the Oval Bed on the north front and dwarf roses in the NE Oval. Jefferson's appointment as Minister in France from 1784 to 1789 led to some botanical exchange there and in December 1802 he asked Robert Bailey to secure seeds and plants for a French friend including 'wild roses of every kind – ½ bushel of each'. Nine months later he wrote to Madame Noailles de Tessé, regretting the delay caused by war and promising to send the wild rose seeds by the Mediterranean route. Some would undoubtedly have been of the 'Cherokee Rose' (*R. laevigata*), grown at Monticello from seeds sent to Jefferson in 1794 by Governor Milledge of Georgia.

Of Philip Miller's works, Jefferson possessed *The Garden Kalendar* (1765), *The Gardeners Dictionary* (1768) and the French edition of this (1785). Judging from his many references to Miller in the *Garden Book*, advice from Chelsea was evidently followed, particularly where growing vegetables was concerned. Appropriate roses for the shrubbery and Poplar Forest were probably noted from the *Dictionary* where, as already mentioned, Miller made much of them for wilderness plantings.

Another *Dictionary* devotee was a skilled gardener of Prestwould, Virginia: Lady Skipwith, second wife of Sir Peyton, who made a wild garden. She grew many native plants, sometimes mentioning, with glee, a discovery *not* to be found in Miller. Heading her list of flowering shrubs was 'a tolerable collection of roses, amongst which are a double and a single yellow rose, Marble and Cabbage Rose'.

One of the oldest houses remaining today in Philadelphia's Germantown Avenue and partly dating from 1689 is Wyck, to which additions were made and the whole reconstructed internally in 1824 for Reuben Haines. His wife, Jane, planted a rose garden and listed over twenty varieties including favourite old Gallicas and Albas, the little Centifolia, 'Pompon de Bourgogne', and Chinas, 'Old Blush' and 'Sanguinea', eighteen of which are grown in the box-bordered beds today.

While in America, consideration should be given to an early breeder, Samuel Feast, a nurseryman of Baltimore who used the native 'Prairie Rose' (then named *R. rubifolia* and now *R. setigera*) to breed some outstanding climbing roses. Soon widely acclaimed, the deep pink 'Queen of the Prairies' was believed to have a Gallica parent. Other successes were 'Baltimore Belle', a very pale blush, almost white, and the red 'King of the Prairies'. John Gray of the Grange Conservatories, Toronto, wrote of these in his 1846 catalogue as 'perfectly hardy, well adapted for planting in front of houses or to train up a veranda' and priced the 'Queen' at 5s, a sum only exceeded by two other new

RIGHT
Damask rose, 'Kazanlik',
long used in Europe for
perfume, was taken to
Western America by
Spanish missionaries.

'Leda' or 'Painted
Damask', praised by
Hovey Nurseries,
Cambridge, Mass, in
1845, well shown at
Mottisfont in 1987.

roses. 'Baltimore Belle' was 2s 6d, the price charged for both by George
Leslie's Toronto Nursery in 1853. Prairie Roses headed the Climbers section
in the catalogue of Hovey's Cambridge Nurseries, Boston in the autumn of
1845, but it is interesting to look at this nursery's old roses in the face of
growing competition from the new varieties.

The long list of Gallicas is divided into 125 self-coloured or shaded varieties
and 176 marbled, spotted, striped or variegated ('some as striped as the
carnation, of surpassing beauty'). 'Boule de Nanteuil' is starred in the first and
'Oillet Parfait' in the second section. Sixteen true 'Provence' or 'Cabbage
Roses' are listed with 'Nelly, blush tinged fawn, beautiful' and 'Sir Walter
Scott, purplish and fine' receiving special mention, while the ever popular
'Unique' is starred. A subdivision named Hybrid Provence totalling fifty, is
described as a 'Class containing very fine roses of beautiful form and delicate
colours, well adapted for showing'. Attention is drawn to 'Rosemary' – a
mottled rose with a pink rosette in the centre. A hundred and one Moss Roses
are an indication of maintained demand with 'no pains or expense spared to
make a complete collection of this most exquisite class'. Twenty-nine Damask,
with 'Madame Hardy' and 'Leda' specially mentioned, twenty-one Alba,
including 'superb Queen of Denmark' and 'exquisite Félicité Parmentier'
complete the extensive Hovey collection of summer-flowering roses, many of
them fairly recent introductions, yet their total was exceeded by the new
remontant varieties.

Roses in the American West had for long been associated with the missions
and it is said that in 1770 Father Junipero Serra was greeted with them on his
arrival in Monterey. Probably the old pink Castilian rose, *R. damascena
trigintipetala*, was included and certainly the white 'Cherokee Rose'
(*R. laevigata*), so well established in the southern states as to banish
recollection of its Chinese origin, would have been used. With the discovery of
gold in California in 1848 and rapid development in the West, all known rose
varieties began to arrive, to blossom with resounding success, Oregon
becoming the state most associated with roses.

In her book *Old Roses* (New York, 1935) Ethelyn Emery Keays includes those of the colonial period, many collected by her in Maryland and others sent to her from various states. She was one of the first to revive an interest in early roses and amongst them, she praises 'Stanwell Perpetual', a chance *R. pimpinellifolia* seedling from Lee of Hammersmith in 1838, for flowering long with delicious sweetness. Her scholarly account, recently reprinted (Heyden, 1978), makes worthwhile reading.

CHAPTER 3

Search in the States

MY garden and other rose commitments keep me in England during the summer and trips abroad are necessarily made in other seasons so that I miss first rose flowerings in the northern hemisphere. However, people and libraries are equally important to my rose story, and in October 1985 I set off for California, firstly to the Huntington Art Gallery and Botanical Gardens in San Marino. When he was horticulturist there, John C. Macgregor IV assembled a comprehensive collection of roses (more than 1,600) and contributed much valuable work on identification and classification of older varieties. His successor, Clair Martin III, and his staff in the Botanical Library gave me welcome guidance with research and I was soon deep in early catalogues of Prince, Hovey and others, always a good source of information on rose distribution.

The Huntington rose garden arrangement is historical, the oldest being in the Herb and Shakespeare Gardens. A substantial pergola, mostly clothed with Noisettes flowering well in October, is flanked by a good collection of Chinas and Teas and many other roses of the nineteenth century. Those of the twentieth century are also grouped chronologically in beds covering a central section, their uniformity broken by decorative archways; a comprehensive selection of species roses is planted on the far side of the garden. In a Rose Study Plot, instituted by John Macgregor, some 224 roses are regimented, ranging from species through older classes to miscellaneous shrubs and shrub-climbers of today, all well documented. The Huntington proved an interesting venue for the Third International Heritage Rose Conference in May 1988.

Further north, in the Atherton area south of San Francisco, I was fortunate to stay with Timmy Gallacher, a prominent member of the Garden Club of America. My bedroom was a veritable library of garden history, the window looking out on her well-planned shade garden of native Californian plants, haunted by hummingbirds. We spent some time at Filoli; this was originally the magnificent home of William Bowers Bourn III, built between 1916 and 1919, with an equally splendid garden dominated by substantial Irish yews, grown from cuttings taken from his family estate near Killarney in Ireland and now providing good background for a well-established broad border of historic roses. Decorative standards break the formality of the main rose garden planting and its neat box hedges.

The Heritage Roses Group had asked me to speak to the North California section and early one morning I was collected by Barbara Worl, her van piled high with rose paraphernalia from Bell's Book Store in Palo Alto. On our way to Merritt College, Oakland, she explained how there was nothing official about the constitution of Heritage Roses Group in America; any member can convene a meeting, provided there is adequate accommodation for a considerable assembly not only of amateur growers of old roses, but also those in any way associated with them – researchers, authors, artists, photographers and nurserymen with a wide selection of their roses in pots. Among the latter at Oakland were Tom Liggett of San Jose, Joyce Demitz of Fort Bragg and Philip Robinson of Sebastapol. The gathering was an all-day affair, crammed with activity; erecting and filling display stands, talking to experts, listening to lectures, snatching a sandwich, buying roses, books or cards and finally dismantling exhibits. People had come from great distances and this gathering of old-rose lovers seemed one of convivial enthusiasm and enjoyment.

Barbara organized a garden tour on another day; first to one she had created, not around her home but in a two-acre section, its house lost through fire. Here, over eighteen years, she had been growing old roses and, even on a misty October morning, midsummer magic lingered. I could appreciate the flowering forms on either side of winding paths, even without their colour, and felt her garden demonstrates respect for roses, almost allowing them to run the show and take credit for their self-arrangement. I was reminded of roses in abandoned abundance at Lime Kiln, Humphrey Brooke's garden in Suffolk.

We went south to the gardens of some people I had met at Oakland: Frances Grate at Pacific Grove and Barbara Palm at Cartmel. The first, with evergreen oak shading fern, fuchsia and begonia, had massed Chinas flowering profusely in full sun and roses with mixed planting in partially shaded beds, making the most of every corner. The second showed a modest collection of roses, carefully integrated with unusual plants and thoughtful touches, like a skep for bees. Finally we saw Betty Dante's garden exposed on a hillside in Salinas, her tenacious roses growing with contrasting foliage plants against a background of 'folded' hills in John Steinbeck country.

Through her own Sweetbrier Press, Barbara Worl has stimulated old-rose appreciation with attractive calendars, cards and booklets. *Garden Open Today: Heritage Rose Gardens* is an excellent up-to-date guidebook for any visitor to the area. One of two outstanding publications is *A Portfolio of Rose Hips* (Palo Alto, 1980), consisting of twelve outstanding watercolours by Jessie Chizu Baer and detailed commentary by John Macgregor. The other ambitious venture of Sweetbrier Press is a facsimile edition (1980) of *Beauties of the Rose*, Henry Curtis (1850–3) with an introduction by Léonie Bell. Her valuable chart showing Curtis roses keyed to other nineteenth-century rose publications also compares dates of introduction with availability in Californian nurseries (1853–62).

Miriam Wilkins is responsible for founding the Heritage Rose Group and is, indeed, its continuing builder. She kindly gave me examples of her circulations since 1972 when, through the *American Rose Magazine*, she asked any lover of old roses to contact her. Response was astonishing and resulted in co-

ABOVE RIGHT
'Madame le Gras de St. Germain', white Alba with hint of yellow, acclaimed by William Paul, 1848, is to be found in the Huntingdon Botanical Gardens.

RIGHT
'Common Moss' appears in records of early American gardens and has been planted at Woodlawn, well restored by the Garden Club of Virginia.

ordinators being appointed for four main regions. The first *Rose Letter*, set out in 1975 on four loose sheets packed with information on both sides, is now produced in booklet form by another editor, although Miriam is still responsible for an *Old Rosers' Digest*, published twice yearly with specific news for her region and exhortations to form sub-groups, rescue old roses and visit gardens. By 1987 her enthusiasm had led to a total membership of over 1,200. I wish I had had time to see her own immense collection of old roses at El Cerrito and also to visit the Nursery of Roses of Yesterday and Today, in Brown's Valley, Watsonville, having caught a glimpse of their roses in an admirable catalogue.

I visited Pennsylvania and Virginia in the East during autumn 1986 and again was fortunate to be staying with the owner of a library of garden history works so comprehensive that it seemed almost unnecessary to go further afield. I first met Elizabeth McLean over the Tercentenary Garden Exhibit from Pennsylvania staged at Chelsea Flower Show in 1982. I had always wanted to visit that state, not least because of the association between Philip Miller and John Bartram (see p. 16) and was delighted to see the American collector's house and garden, the oldest botanical one in the USA, originally set in countryside, but now on the outskirts of Philadelphia. A drawing of the property 'as it appears from the River, 1758' and sent by Bartram to Philip Collinson, shows a 'new Flower garden' extending 25 yds (25 m) from his study window and I felt roses from Chelsea would have been planted there. Perhaps in the larger 'Common Flower Garden' native roses collected by Bartram on his travels grew and maybe swamp roses flourished down by the River Schuylkill, where precious packages would have arrived from another Physic Garden far away by the Thames. When working at the library of the Pennsylvania Horticultural Society, I gleaned rose information from their own early records and also from *Gardens of Colony and State*, vol II by Alice G. Lockwood (1931), where I found a charming illustration of a two-storey pergola swathed in roses and used for dancing. From it, revellers would look down on massed colour in formal box-edged rose beds, laid out around 1820 for the owners of Perry Hall, nr Easton, Maryland by Kercheval, a gardener from England.

I was pleased to meet Léonie Bell and could appreciate her dedication to and knowledge of old roses. With Lily Shohan, she was instrumental in urging the important reprinting of eleven scarce books (New York, 1978), five English books – Bunyard, Gore, Lindley, Paul, Rivers – and six American – Buist, Ellwanger, Keays, Parsons, Prince and Shepherd – thus providing easy access for all those interested in classic works. With Helen Van Pelt Wilson, Léonie produced *The Fragrant Year* (New York, 1967), her chapter on rose scents being a wonderful exercise in nose-detection and the book contains her lovely illustrations. These and her writings are widely published, including a contribution to *The Rose Annual* (1983). I spent a morning with Judy McKeon, horticulturist/rosarian at the Morris Arboretum, University of Pennsylvania, who maintains an immaculate rose garden there. Forty-three symmetrical beds are planted with acclaimed varieties of striking shades and away from this main complex, informal Rugosas, species and modern shrub roses are grown. Among them 'Bonica', a recent Meilland introduction, demonstrates a change in rose appreciation, it being the first shrub rose ever to gain the All-America Rose Selections Award among the best new roses for 1987. Judy told me she would like to see more old varieties in the garden and I suggested some late Victorian and Edwardian favourites which the founders, John T. Morris and his sister, might have planted when this area was part of Compton, their country estate, to be viewed from the seclusion of Lydia's seat above.

An enclosed rose garden at Dumbarton Oaks, Washington, was a favoured spot of owners Mr and Mrs Robert Woods Bliss early in this century. They too, used a special seat for contemplation of the formal beds offset by trim, low box hedges and bushes. I had been given permission to work in the library there over the weekend. Although it was disappointing to find the renowned collection of rare horticultural books inaccessible owing to redecoration, in the general library I found more early catalogues, and scoured copies of *The Horticulturist and Journal of Rural Art and Rural Taste*, as well as the *American Journal of Horticulture and Florist's Companion*, for rose references. I found some commending Thomas Rivers, the English rose grower. An interesting article of 1861 on imported roses encouraged growers to work on propagation and quoted the example of 'Madame Trudeaux Rose'. Originally from Bloomingdale, New York, it was given a French name and sent to France, where it became known the world over before the USA could be induced to import it. This article stressed that French stock was poor, English plants often suffered through a change from a cool moist climate to a hot, dry one; therefore it would be far more economic to produce roses at home.

A chance meeting with Dorothy Miller from Front Royal, Virginia, at a Garden History Society gathering at Stoke-on-Trent led to an invitation to speak to her Garden Club of Warren County. She took me south to the Rose Show of the Garden Club of Virginia at Fredericksburg where I was given a copy of *Historic Virginia Gardens* by Dorothy Hunt Williams (Charlottesville,

Floriculture of the toilet, in *The Gardeners Magazine*, 1851 decreed a Rose or Camellia for evening wear.

1974). This provides explicit documentation of important preservation work by the club and features listings of plants, including roses, used in restoring gardens. At Woodlawn, the house built by Nelly (née Custis) and Lawrence Lewis on ground given them in 1799 by their relative George Washington, two parterres have been recreated and planted predominantly with roses known in the early nineteenth century, favourite flowers of the Lewis family. Under the club's auspices, some of the Jefferson roses already referred to are growing again at Monticello, while at Gunston Hall, overlooking the Potomac – 'one of the most beautiful boxwood gardens in America', established by the Masons in the late eighteenth century – early roses are well displayed against sculptured evergreen.

Many old roses were planted in the Hollywood Cemetery, Richmond, VA: these were carved on a tombstone a hundred years ago.

Three rewarding days in Richmond, efficiently organized by Dorothy's daughter, Elaine, included researching at the Library of the Historical Society of Virginia, seeking old roses in the Hollywood Cemetery and visiting varied gardens. Appropriate roses and herbs are planted in the walled garden of Agecroft, a fifteenth- to sixteenth-century house transported from Cheshire in England in the 1920s, and they top splendid Italian terraces on pergola and balustrade at a Victorian house called Maymont. Bob Cromey works wonders with tenacious roses on a steep, stony site and a most exciting collection is to be found in the garden of Marie and John Butler at Chesterfield.

Interesting Cromey roses have come from varied sources: unknown Americans from Mrs Watkins of North Carolina include 'Steeple Rose', 'Prince Albert' and 'Jacotte', a lovely apricot-pink Rambler planted in the remains of a rotten oak log. Others are imported from Lykkes of Denmark, Huber of Switzerland, Beales of England and Pickering of Ontario, a Canadian nursery with a good range of Gallicas, a most tolerant class, only occasionally paling at the testing soil and climatic conditions. In June, July and August temperatures can soar to over 100°F (37°C) and except for climbers ('Sombreuil' flourishes, as in the heat of California) there is little flowering. Many of the old roses lose foliage, but new growth survives and is maintained until mid-October. In England we should count our blessings; recent excessively cold winter spells and wet summers have not unduly disturbed the majority of our roses.

The Butlers rank high among enthusiasts I have met in my travels and I asked how they became involved with old roses. They replied:

Our interest grew out of twenty-two years of growing and using many varieties of herbs. The old writings about the making of pot pourri proved fascinating and led to an investigation and acquisition of some old roses most suitable for this purpose. Later, an article in *The Rose Letter* by Carl Cato on 'Tea Roses in the South' compelled us to include these beauties in our plantings. Here in central Virginia at the northernmost limit of their survival, we have found many of these treasures of yesteryear in our excursions to historical sites, plantations and old cemeteries. But again, it proved to be the herbs and the early herbalists which inspired our search for a very special rose. Having read and re-read Gerard, Parkinson, Herrman and others on roses of their day, we found Graham Stuart Thomas's writings on the musk rose especially appealing. Thus *Rosa moschata* became the rose to captivate our greatest interest. Steeped in seventeenth- and eighteenth-century gardening history, could not the Commonwealth of Virginia yield a treasured remnant of this very special *Rosa*

LEFT

Californian nursery, Roses of Yesterday and Today, lists fragrant 'Félicité Parmentier' as one of the loveliest Albas.

moschata? The description we committed to memory. When Ruth Knopf brought a small plant of an unknown rose grown from a cutting from a cemetery in North Carolina, we felt certain it was worthy of closer investigation. After two years of studying and observing the several plants we subsequently acquired, we feel certain that, indeed, *Rosa moschata* is alive and well, not only in England, but also in the Southern United States. We continue our correspondence with people in various parts of the United States to determine *Rosa moschata*'s growth and flower habits in different climatic areas.

I hope this may lead to exchange of information further afield.

By late afternoon it was marginally cooler at Chesterfield, some twenty miles south of Richmond, and it was delightful to wander with Charles Walker from North Carolina, Bob Cromey and others through the Butlers' well-planned garden. Herb and vegetable areas have been incorporated with broad borders of roses laid out on central axes, with clever under-planting, complementary shrubs and infilling bulbs. Marie is adamant in maintaining year-round interest, not only in winter, but also in the 'bleak period of heat and insects' between the great rose flush in May and repeating varieties in late summer and autumn. Polyanthas, Teas and Chinas were flowering, many unfamiliar to me and some of which had not yet been firmly identified. There was no mistaking rampant, grey-purple foliage, though, and I at once recognized 'Sir Cedric Morris', discovered by him as a chance *R. glauca* hybrid in his Suffolk garden, here revelling in a distant, warmer climate. After a splendid tea, including shortbread with sweet cecily imprint and cake made with rose oil, we all contributed to a slide show and I was urged to include mine of 'Perle d'Or' in this book (see p. 67).

Charles Walker is co-ordinator of the Heritage Roses Group in the South-East and in 1987 he sent me details of the Heritage Rose Foundation, an international organization set up by him and others, with an aim to collect and preserve heritage roses and promote their culture by establishing gardens and a comprehensive rose research library. The first issue of *Heritage Rose Foundation News*, April 1987, advocated a practice used in Bermuda to allow unidentified roses to be exhibited. Peter Harkness suggested that a special class for them should be instituted, enabling visiting experts to make an assessment.

Some of Bermuda's 'mystery' roses are illustrated in a small book, *Old Garden Roses in Bermuda* (1984), published by the Bermuda Rose Society, founded in 1954 and primarily interested in 'the old-fashioned roses that have stood the test of time in these islands'. Many were brought by ships calling from both East and West routes and in 1956 the locally known 'Belfield Rose' was identified as the original 'Slater's Crimson China'. The Bermuda Rose Society recognizes the importance of an international organization concerned with the conservation of old roses and was the first to make a substantial contribution to the Heritage Rose Foundation. (For details, see Appendix II.)

Part II

CHINA'S CONTRIBUTION

Without interruption the flowers bloom and fade
Regardless of the coming and going of spring.

SU SHI (1037–1101)
(Famous poet of the Sung Dynasty on Monthly Roses)

'Old Blush China'.

CHAPTER 4

Roses from Nursery Gardens and the Wild

AN early record of the rose in China dates from the Han Dynasty, when the Emperor Hanwudy (*c.* 140 BC) judged the Monthly Rose (Chang Wei) to be more beautiful than the smile of his most esteemed concubine. This rose, frequently reproduced on porcelain and silk, appears very similar to our 'Old Blush China' of today. By the seventeenth century, towards the end of the Ming and the beginning of the Qing dynasties, the number of garden roses had increased considerably. Later it was considered important to select and record some of the most outstanding classic varieties. These were summarized in a book, a copy of which is in the possession of a famous family of horticulturists – the Shens, in Wuxi; I was fortunate to meet Y. C. Shen in San Francisco where he practises his great skill in creating miniature *penjing* (*bonsai*). When he heard about my plans for a book, he obtained more details of this Chinese work; I include a précis below of a translation of part of it. Through textual research, the Shens have established that the book *Variety of Roses* was probably published during the time of Emperor Jia Qing (1796–1820) for private circulation in Yang Zhou, not far from Shanghai, under the pseudonym of Pin Hua Guan Zhu (Master of Flower Reviewer).

> With the development of the fertile Yang Zhou area in the Yangtse River Valley and consequent inducement for a number of influential people to settle there, came an increase in life's embellishments, including roses evolved through hybridization. Poets and painters named them according to their characteristics and this book describes ten considered most rare and precious among the thousands available at the time. 'Lan Tian Bi' gains its name from exquisite jade used for ceremonial purposes: 'Lan' (blue) describes the shade of a few petals in the centre of the flower. A golden bird splashing in water gives to another rose the name of 'Jin Ou Fan Lu'. One called 'Kuo Guo Dan Zhuang' is reminiscent of the Queen of Kuo Guo, charmingly dressed, while 'Yu Shi Zhuang' represents the colourful robes of a Taoist priest. A flying, flame-breathing red dragon of Chinese mythology gives its name to a new dark red rose 'Chi Long Han Zhu', its centre petals tightly curled, like the pearl this monster always keeps in its mouth. A pink rose, 'Liu Zhao Jin Fen' is as tender and delicate as a beautiful girl in an ancient palace and a paler bloom, neither white nor pink, but shaded between the two, gains the name of 'Shui Yue Zhuang' to describe a lovely girl combing her long hair by a pool, the moon reflected in the water. Petals edged with a tint of red surround a greyish-white rose named 'Xiao Feng Chan Yue' to convey a picturesque scene of dawning day, with a cool, gentle breeze as the moon pales in the sky. 'Bolumi' with a light yellow bloom, resembles the flesh of a fruit called 'Bolu' and, finally, 'Chun Shui Lu Bo', a pale green rose, gains its name from water gently disturbed by rain and breezes in spring.

These were the ten treasured roses of subtle shade and evocative name – pale as the moon or fiery as a dragon – and Mr Shen tells me that he grew the second, 'Jin Ou Fan Lu' in his Wuxi garden and that its yellow blooms had a kind of 'light green, cold feeling'. This demonstrates the accuracy of description in these poetic Chinese names.

Alongside their many cultivars, often grown in pots, species roses indigenous to China, Japan and Korea had for long been used in garden decoration. For example, in early spring vigorous *R. multiflora* would hang large clusters of tiny white flowers over garden pavilion or monumental rock, treasured for sculptured shape worked by erosion. Early variations of this rose were *R. m. carnea* and deeper *R. cathayensis* which might have been used to cover bamboo treillage and provide a decorative wall between garden compartments. Another species used in Far Eastern gardens and also appearing in many early illustrations was *R. rugosa*. This flowered long, either white, pink or magenta, and was also valued for its deep-veined foliage in gardens where texture contrast was important and conspicuous red fruit would provide autumn colour. Before the turn of the eighteenth century, some species from China travelled far afield.

The vigorous invasion of the southern states of the USA by China's

R. laevigata has been mentioned and in 1793 an interesting species reached England: *R. bracteata* was brought back by Lord Macartney on his return from a diplomatic mission to China. Included in his staff was George Staunton, a keen botanist and gardener, who later established one of the first gardens in England to emphasize Chinese features at Leigh Park in Hampshire, where he might have grown the 'Macartney Rose', as it is also known. Leigh Park is being carefully restored today under the auspices of the Hampshire Gardens Trust and I hope that *R. bracteata* will be planted in a sheltered spot to display large single white flowers over a long period. This rose gains its botanical name from prominent leafy bracts and it also has unusually blunted ends to its leaves. Banksian roses were brought from China to England at the beginning of the nineteenth century, named for the wife of collector and botanist, Sir Joseph Banks, but the vast wealth of China's wild roses was not uncovered until towards the end of the century. Before looking at intrepid collectors of the time, the introduction of Chinese roses to the West must be considered.

There had been spasmodic appearances in Europe earlier: Gronovius, a Dutch botanist, included one in his herbarium of 1733 and twenty years later another reached Sweden, of which a dried specimen exists in the Linnaean collection. *The Gardeners' Chronicle* of 5 May 1854, contributed an interesting observation from the *Memoirs* of the Baroness d'Oberkirch, dating from a visit in 1782:

R. bracteata, introduced by Lord Macartney from China in 1793, was used by William Paul to produce 'Mermaid' in 1918.

> I was delighted with Haarlem, a beautiful city, and we saw the gardener who is celebrated through Europe and a shrub which produced beautiful flowers, petals soft as velvet, but odourless. He told us it was the Chinese Rose and had been imported within the last year with great care. Roses of this species may, in fact, be seen delineated on screens and in corners of fans.

This would probably have been the old Blush China rose, well illustrated in a painting on silk, reproduced in *Old Garden Roses*, by Edward Bunyard (London, 1936). I took a photograph of one in my own garden, with a bud, and the similarity with the other picture, a thousand years before, is quite extraordinary, almost petal for petal.

There was only one area where foreigners were allowed to collect plants in China around the turn of the eighteenth century, and that was devoted to nursery gardens near Canton, the port for merchant shipping. Officials of the East India Company resided in Macao and, no doubt, filled their gardens with potted plants from Fa Tee (the Flowery Land), situated on an island suburb across the Pearl River to the south-west of Canton. Later, Ernest Wilson wrote, 'our early knowledge of the Chinese flora was based on plants procured from gardens, notably from those around Canton'. An article by Ng Yong-Sang in the *China Journal*, XX, 4 (Shanghai, April 1934), tells of local legend regarding the origin of this land of flowers. At the time of the Five Dynasties (907–960), a member of the house of Liu reigned over the southern part, with Canton his capital. When his favourite concubine died, he wished her, Su Hsing, to be buried on an uninhabited island nearby. Over her grave grew a new species of flower with a wonderful fragrance, decreed by the ruler to be named Hy Hsing (jasmine). Later it spread all over the island and visitors were entranced, some settling there to grow other flowers and establish a new industry. The name Fa Tee was bestowed on this fertile area, which became a flower market for the city and attracted many visitors, especially over the New Year holiday.

John Livingstone, an employee of the East India Company living in Macao, reported to the Horticultural Society of London in November 1819 that 'The state of botany in China may be pretty correctly understood by examining the Fa Tee Flower Gardens ... it is from these nurseries that Europeans are generally supplied with the plants which they send or carry home.' However, the Chinese guarded their produce carefully and did not allow ready access; by 1819 foreign visitors were restricted to two or three days a month with a fee of $8 a time. All plants were grown in pots, supplied to the wealthy Chinese for instant flowering through the seasons, spring bulbs being replaced by peonies, peonies by roses, roses by chrysanthemums, so that there was a constant succession of bloom in the gardens where walls, paving, covered walks and little pavilions needed brightening. Sometimes the potted plants were placed in ceramic containers supplying additional colour. The soil of the area, strong alluvial clay, was used at Fa Tee for their plants and was not at all suitable, Livingstone considered, for a long sea voyage. He advised repotting in good soil, tending carefully for at least six months before sailing and above all, the plants should be in the hands of someone who knew how to care for them – John Reeves, for instance.

Reeves was a tea inspector for the East India Company and in 1819 he brought ninety of 100 plants safely back to England. But live plants were not his only contribution to the West's knowledge of Chinese flora; he arranged for Chinese artists to work in his own home and under his supervision faithfully to reproduce many of the ornamental plants available at the time. It is fair conjecture to assume that the majority would have come from the Fa Tee Nursery Gardens and the valuable collection, in four volumes, may be seen today in the Lindley Library of the Royal Horticultural Society. Fifteen roses, both species and garden varieties, are included and whenever I see them I am impressed by the pristine colour and can well imagine the interest they would have aroused when first seen. They are also an indication that trade in roses was flourishing at Fa Tee; here could be purchased, *R. multiflora* and *R. microphylla*, the 'Monthly Blush' and the 'Monthly Red', *R. indica*, double white and double yellow, the yellow Banksia, and, somewhat surprising, a large double pink 'Centifolia type' and a double purple. This was almost a preview of the roses to become so important in the nineteenth century throughout the world.

After retiring from his work in China and settling in England, John Reeves gave much time to the Horticultural Society and was instrumental in organizing Robert Fortune's first expedition to China in 1843. In the previous year the Treaty of Nanking had given Britain more trade facilities and opened up areas for botanical collection inland from the ports of Hong Kong, Amoy, Fuchou, Ningpo and Shanghai. In the lengthy directive for their collector, the Society considered it desirable to draw his attention to twenty-two items, among them the 'Double Yellow Roses' (perhaps noted from the Reeves collection) 'of which two sorts are said to occur in Chinese gardens, exclusive of the Banksian'.

From his account *Three Years Wandering in China* (London, 1847) Fortune tells of visiting the Canton area in 1844, when he 'lost no time in visiting the celebrated Fa Tee Nurseries ... from whence a great number of those fine plants were first produced which now decorate our gardens in England'. There were about a dozen nurseries, smaller than any in London at that time, with plants mostly in large pots lining narrow paved walks, but there were also stock grounds for plants and for the first process of dwarfing trees, the art of *bonsai*, originating with the Chinese. He found them generally 'gay with the tree paeony, azalea, camellias and roses', but the garden formerly belonging to the East India Company was then in rather a sorry state. As it was the time of the Chinese New Year (18 February), he described the festivities: streets, temples, houses and boats lavishly decorated with flowers brought down from the hills and fireworks adding sparkle to the occasion.

In Ningpo Fortune visited gardens belonging to mandarins, containing 'new plants of great beauty and interest' and

> on entering one of the gardens on a fine morning in May, I was struck with a mass of yellow flowers which completely covered a distant part of the wall. The colour was not a common yellow, but had something of buff in it, which gave the flowers a striking uncommon appearance. I immediately ran up to the place and, to my surprise and delight, found that it was a most *beautiful new double yellow climbing rose*. I have no doubt, from what I afterwards learned, that this rose is from the more northern districts of the empire and will prove perfectly hardy in Europe. Another rose, which the Chinese call 'Five Coloured', was also found in one of these gardens at the time. It belongs to the section commonly called the China roses in this country [England], but grows in a very strange and beautiful manner. Sometimes it produces self-coloured blooms, being either red or French white and frequently having flowers of both on one plant at the same time – while at other times the flowers are striped with two of the colours. This will also be as hardy as our common China Rose.

Roses were once grown in this little enclosed garden in the Fa Tee Nursery area – one possibly visited by Livingstone, Reeves and Fortune.

Drawing of *R. microphylla* from the Reeves's
collection. This rose came to Calcutta Botanic
Garden from Canton, to be named *R. roxburgii
roxburgii.*

ABOVE RIGHT   *R. moyesii*, discovered by E. H.
Wilson in Western China, makes a 12 feet bush,
spectacular with flagon-shaped hips in early autumn.

RIGHT   Brilliant blooms of 'Canary Bird',
descended from China's *R. xanthina*, well displayed
with light ferny foliage in early summer.

Actually, the first, which came to be known as 'Fortune's Yellow', did not prove hardy in England, but the beautiful loose flowers, tinged with orange, caused some excitement and were displayed to advantage in conservatories. The second was probably *R. multiflora* 'Grevillei', or *R. multiflora platyphylla*, known in the West as 'Seven Sisters Rose', for its many shades varying from purple to white and introduced earlier from the Far East by Sir Charles Greville. In Shanghai Fortune found a garden variety of *R. rugosa*, rich purple and sweetly scented, and also a beautiful double white rose, thought to be a hybrid between *R. banksiae* and *R. laevigata*, one to prove robust as an understock, known as *R. × fortuniana*.

By the late nineteenth century, botanical expeditions were penetrating far into China and many more exciting discoveries were made. With foliage, flowers and fruit of great diversity, these species roses soon travelled worldwide, some to become important in the breeding of new shrub roses of the twentieth century. E. H. Wilson, a collector for Kew (sponsored by the Veitch Nursery) and for the Arnold Arboretum in America, vividly describes a rose scene in western Hupeh, country of the dramatic Yangtse gorges.

> Rose bushes abound everywhere and in April perhaps afford the greatest show of any one kind of flower. *R. laevigata* and *R. microcarpa* are more common in fully exposed places. *R. multiflora*, *R. moschata* and *R. banksiae* are particularly abundant on the cliffs and crags of the glens and gorges, though by no means confined thereto. The Musk and Banksian Roses often scale tall trees and a tree thus festooned with their branches laden with flowers is a sight to be remembered. To walk through a glen in the early morning or after a slight shower, when the air is laden with the soft delicious perfume from myriads of rose flowers, is truly a walk through an earthly paradise.
>
> *A Naturalist in Western China* (London, 1913)

(The *R. moschata* referred to here by Wilson is, in fact, *R. brunonii*, the Himalayan Musk Rose and not the old *R. moschata* of Miller. They are often confused and the whole matter is thoroughly explained by Graham Thomas in *Climbing Roses Old and New*, London 1965, pp. 48–57.)

We owe much to Wilson for many valuable rose introductions and I will take three rewarding examples of different habit, all most decorative in a larger garden. *R. willmottiae*, with arching form, makes a good bush of about 6 ft (1·8 m), with dark stems and rather greyish-green ferny foliage, well offsetting single lilac-pink flowers, followed by small pear-shaped red hips in the autumn. *R. moyesii*, rated by Graham Thomas as one of Wilson's greatest treasures from the Far East, grows taller: up to 12 ft (3·6 m) to display vivid crimson single flowers wonderfully against a blue sky in the early summer. But perhaps most decorative of any rose fruit are this rose's splendid pendulous flagon-shaped hips, borne in abundance and making a vivid orange-red display in early autumn. Wilson named this species to mark his appreciation of hospitality received from a missionary in China, the Rev J. Moyes. For his wife he named a very beautiful climbing one *R. helenae*, which will reach 20 ft (6 m) or more and is well grown through a tree to cascade heavy white corymbs of bloom in late July – after the majority of species roses. These are followed by full hanging bunches of orange hips, in my garden the very last to be taken by the birds, and I have seen them powdered with snow, sparkling in the sun at Christmas time.

A French missionary, Père David, was collecting in China at the end of the nineteenth century and later *R. davidii* was named for him. This species does not seem to be grown often, but I find it useful, flowering late in July and not too invasive for the smaller garden. In 1908 Frank Meyer, a collector from the USA, introduced the double yellow *R. xanthina* from northern China and in the following year, the single variety, *R. × spontanea*. This was known in China as 'the Yellow Prickly Rose' and now a descendant of it is the universal favourite, 'Canary Bird', one of the first roses to brighten our gardens in late spring. Reginald Farrer, the Yorkshire plant hunter particularly interested in alpines, found in the Ta-tung Mountains, north of Sining, a rose from which a later seedling was noticed in 1914 by E. A. Bowles, to be named appropriately, 'Threepenny Bit Rose' (*R. elegantula* 'Persetosa'). With tiny salmon-pink flowers and delicate ferny foliage turning attractively reddish in the autumn, it makes a 6 ft (1·8 m) bush of rather daintier appearance than many other species roses.

I have chosen a few of China's wild roses to illustrate their charm and diversity from the many collected around the beginning of this century, but the original *R. chinensis*, from which all early Chinese garden roses must have evolved, long remained elusive. Before I went to China in 1981, the late Sir John Keswick sent me a copy of an account by Dr Augustine Henry (*The Gardeners' Chronicle*, June 1903) of its discovery in Hupeh some eighteen years earlier, together with notes of his own expedition to this area in 1979 and his attempts to rediscover this historic rose. He brought back five varieties from Ichang and Chengtu, but although some resemblance was acknowledged, doubt still remained. In 1986 we were shown a photograph of the single pink *R. chinensis var. spontanea*, discovered in western China by a Japanese researcher in 1983. I advise everyone interested in the parentage of our roses to read one of the accounts by Graham Thomas, published in *The Rose* (journal of the Royal National Rose Society, September 1986) or in *The Garden* (journal of the Royal Horticultural Society, March 1987), acclaiming the work of Mr Mikinori Ogisu in rediscovering this missing link, which led directly to the earliest Chinese garden roses, the Four Stud Chinas (see p. 42) and their progeny. Perhaps we should echo the thought of Edward Bunyard who concluded his chapter on the rose in China (*Old Garden Roses*): 'There might well be in some English Garden a memorial to the unknown Chinese cultivators to whom we owe so much'.

I would like to add a note of appreciation of 'one of the Nestors of horticulture', as John Reeves was lamented in an obituary notice (*The Gardeners' Chronicle*, 1856), in obtaining all-important blooms from Fa Tee and organizing their faithful reproduction in pictures undoubtedly to arouse curiosity and encourage subsequent pursuit of roses in China.

CHAPTER 5

Chinese Ancestors and their Descendants

COLLECTION of garden roses from China was helped by the nursery gardens' practice of planting their wares in pots, especially if Livingstone's advice on soil replacement was followed and Reeves's directives on sea transport noted. Visitors to the Fa Tee nurseries would have observed roses flowering on into the autumn, among them one with small deep crimson blooms. This was known to have been in Italy earlier than 1792, the date of its arrival in England when it was introduced by Mr Gilbert Slater of Leytonstone and became known as 'Slater's Crimson China'. A figure appeared in Curtis's *Botanical Magazine* two years later. The colour of this little rose was intense, more so than any other rose at that time and, widely disseminated, there is some belief that all red long-flowering roses today owe something to 'Slater's Crimson'.

The next important arrival was a pink China rose, believed to have been brought back by the Macartney expedition in the first instance and passed to Kew. It was named 'Parsons's Pink' in 1793 after its grower in Rickmansworth. The following year it was distributed by Colvill's Nursery in King's Road, Chelsea, and quickly crossed the English Channel and the Atlantic, to play a significant part in further rose developments.

The third historic China rose to arrive in England had been procured from the Fa Tee Gardens by John Reeves for Alexander Hume, in charge of the East India Office in Canton, who sent plants to his cousins, Sir Abraham and Lady Hume, keen gardeners in Hertfordshire. Their overseas plants were grown on for them by James Colvill and he introduced 'Hume's Blush Tea-Scented China' in 1810. The following year, in spite of the Napoleonic Wars, raging between England and France, this beautiful rose was safely conveyed to the Empress Joséphine at Malmaison. Although in 1823 John Parks was sent primarily to collect chrysanthemums from China for the Horticultural Society, he was, as we have seen, also given instructions regarding roses and he returned the following year with two: the yellow Banksian (*R. banksiae lutea*) and a full yellow double, to be named 'Parks's Yellow Tea-Scented China'. This was to have a far-reaching effect on the colour of subsequent roses and, with the previous three, this quartet became known as the 'Four Stud Chinas' through the work of Dr C. C. Hurst, 1941 (see Graham Thomas, *The Old Shrub Roses*, London, 1955, pp. 76–80).

That China roses were still offered for sale in containers in Western nurseries is evident from a list issued by Henry Hammond of Bagshot, Surrey for 1827–8. There the 'Dark Red China' is the only rose specifically mentioned 'in pots' for 10s a dozen, twice the price of most other varieties. (I am indebted for this information to the Trustees of the Wedgwood Museum, Barlaston, Stoke-on-Trent and to Keele University Library where the manuscript is deposited.) Thomas Rivers, visiting Paris, was entranced by the sight of hundreds of the yellow Tea for sale in flower markets during summer and

ABOVE RIGHT
'Parks's Yellow Tea-Scented China', here flowering in my Hampshire garden, had a profound effect on new roses of the nineteenth century.

RIGHT
One of the loveliest of the Noisettes, 'Alister Stella Gray', raised in England, 1894, flowers from July to October on my garden wall.

Compact China hybrid, 'Hermosa' produces lilac-pink cupped blooms over a long period; an excellent rose for the small garden.

autumn, 'in pots, with their heads partially enveloped in coloured paper in such an elegant and effective mode that it is scarcely possible to avoid being tempted to give two or three francs for such a pretty object'.

Variations of these roses soon appeared: 'Cramoisi Supérieur' in 1832, a most beautiful rose for small beds as Thomas Rivers stressed in his *Rose Amateur's Guide* and even thirty years on remarked, 'We have not even now any [China] rose more beautiful than 'Cramoisi Supérieur'; its flowers are so finely formed, its crimson tints so rich'. 'Fabvier' (1832) slightly shorter and more inclined to scarlet and 'Hermosa' (1840) a clear pink, more cupped than 'Parsons's', were used in pot culture, proving admirable for the 'window garden'. On 4 December 1838, John Lindley, then secretary of the Horticultural Society, read a paper on the effects of the great frosts of 1837–8, when most China roses were destroyed. By the next decade, when grown as low standards, advice on protection was quoted in reviews of catalogues in *The Gardeners' Chronicle*, 23 September 1848: 'Take up at the end of November, place against a wall with roots in the ground and heads resting against the wall, over which a mat must be nailed in severest weather. Plant out towards the end of March' (Rivers's *Descriptive Catalogue*). With low-growers, it was 'advisable to Protect China and Tea-Scented Roses with a thick layer of decayed tan and small branches of Spruce Fir stuck in the ground a short distance from stools. This will greatly assist in checking severity of frosts'. (William Wood, Maresfield, Sussex.)

Today, I find that well-established China roses need no protection, but even in the south of England I swathe small new plants with dry bracken to protect not only new stems but roots also against long periods of severe weather. 'Arethusa', with lovely yellow shades and 'Irene Watts', with many tints of pink, are two rewarding Chinas of later introduction and, for impact of their delicate shades, are best planted in groups of three. However, I have still to find one approaching 'Old Blush' for providing silvery-pink blooms almost continuously from May to the first frosts. The foliage of these China roses is quite different from leaves of the old roses, being tinged reddish-brown, shining and pointed, on red stems with prominent, curved red prickles, decorative, I think, even before the flowers appear. They are eminently suitable for the smaller garden and can still be grown successfully in pots where space is even more limited.

Perhaps in a consignment from Fa Tee for the Humes, a dwarf variety of 'Parsons's Pink' appeared in the Colvill Nursery in 1805 and led to further variations: dark crimson 'Gloire des Lawrancianas' proving one of the best. These 'Fairy Roses', as they were then called, were soon incorporated in the rose garden, used instead of box or turf for edging gravel walks and supplying buds from April to November. Forced, they could be in flower all winter and were considered the 'best thing at that season for helping out the bouquets' (*The Gardeners' Chronicle*, 29 July 1843). Another development occurred in France early in the nineteenth century, when Boursault Roses were named for an enthusiastic amateur rose grower and, although first believed to have evolved from *R. chinensis* × *R. alpina*, there is now some doubt about this parentage. 'Crimson Boursault' or 'Amadis' has clusters of purplish, rather tousled flowers and associates very happily with pink 'Madame de Sancy de Parabère' of like form. Both are thornless and produce blooms on graceful, arching stems, pleasingly displayed against a mellowed wall.

The Four Stud Chinas were responsible for the rise of five main groups of roses in the West over the greater part of the nineteenth century: Portland, Noisette, Bourbon, Tea and Hybrid Perpetual. There had been some dissention over the origin of the first, possibly named for the second Duchess of Portland, a knowledgeable horticulturist. However, elucidation may now be found in W. J. Bean, *Trees and Shrubs Hardy in the British Isles*, vol 4, eighth edition, London, 1970, a work containing invaluable information on the rose generally. Others of the class followed and are reliable today for fairly compact habit and long flowering quality. I remember visiting the rose garden at Castle Howard one October and being arrested by a show of pink in the distance. This turned out to be 'Comte de Chambord' and I would advise anyone with a small garden to grow it with two more pink Portland Roses, 'Jacques Cartier' of clear bright pink shades and 'Marbrée', mottled deep pink, for a dividend-paying trio. They are all full petalled and the first two delightfully fragrant. If a dwarf decorative hedge is needed, maybe between flowers and vegetables, then the semi-double 'Portland Rose' of compact growth will prove admirable, providing colour over a long period. However, as the buds are tightly placed on a short flower stalk, dead-heading is imperative for optimum effect of the bright crimson flowers, echoing 'The Apothecary's Rose', among the clear green foliage of many old roses.

'Parsons's Pink', or 'Old Blush China', proved a roving and prolific parent producing two important classes, one to emanate from South Carolina and the other from Réunion in the Indian Ocean. In his *Manual of Roses* (New York, 1846), William Prince describes how John Champneys, a Charleston rice planter and 'an eminent and liberal votary of Flora' raised from seed of the old 'White Musk' (*R. moschata*) fertilized by the 'Pink China', a new rose, 'Champneys' Pink Cluster'. The Prince Nursery was presented with two tubs of six plants in each, from which a great many were raised, some sent to France and England. Philippe Noisette, a French nurseryman in Charleston, used the Champneys rose to raise 'Old Blush Noisette', sent it to his brother, Louis, in Paris and soon all leading growers in France were introducing Noisettes.

The most spectacular of them were obtained through the use of 'Parks's

'Comte de Chambord', rewarding Portland rose with deep pink, rather flat flowers, here seen at Castle Howard, Yorkshire in October.

Yellow' and in 1843, when Thomas Rivers was in Angers, he became euphoric over the new 'Cloth of Gold' or 'Chromatella', describing the flowers as a mass of large, golden balls. He also mentioned receiving one of its yellow seedlings, 'Isabella Gray', raised by Mr Gray, a Charleston florist, in 1844. Robert Buist, American rose expert and author of *The Rose Manual* (Philadelphia, 1844) was in Vibert's nursery near Paris in 1839 and was charmed by 'Aimée Vibert', a white Noisette named after the grower's daughter, and one to bloom profusely in the autumn throughout the southern USA, but proving not entirely hardy in Philadelphia. He remarked on the 'charm of colour' in 'Chromatella' making it very desirable to both the French and English and added, 'Plants have not yet bloomed with us, but will do so in March or April, 1844' – just a year after its introduction in France. Buist also pointed out that the white 'Lamarque' was widely known and would grow some 20 ft (6 m) a season in a good dry rich soil. During an Address on Horticulture in 1851 at Macon, Georgia, mention was made of the 'naturally good soil of our state, with vegetable manure from the woods. Upon such compost I have a "Cloth of Gold" rose which covered in two years the greater part of the front of the house, 25 feet [7·5 m] from the ground and a "La Marck", whose stem was in three years the size of a man's wrist'. These few examples will show how rapidly the Noisettes were travelling back and forth across the Atlantic in the first half of the nineteenth century and how quickly they became established, comparatively recently after the arrival in the West of the beautiful yellow Tea-Scented Rose from China.

Today their graceful growth and lasting blooms make them most rewarding climbers. 'Madame Alfred Carrière', a slightly blushing white, will flower well on a north wall, although 'Cloth of Gold' needs protection in the English climate. One bred in England, 'Alister Stella Gray' (1894) has deep yellow buds opening paler and is particularly floriferous in the autumn. Mine was cut back by two cold winters, but has survived, although another planted at the same time in a small sheltered garden off London's Vincent Square, did not suffer and, almost too invasive, has covered three walls. I think apricot 'Crépuscule', of more moderate growth, would be a better choice for a small town garden, or 'William Allen Richardson', named for an American, raised in France (1878) and unusually shaded orange.

Although the Île de Bourbon has for long been credited with the chance cross between the old Damask 'Four Seasons' and the 'Old Blush China', producing the locally named 'Rose Edouard' and subsequent development of Bourbon roses in France, there is another claim from India (see p. 124). Thomas Rivers thought he had the correct story – from M. Bréon, a French botanist, as follows:

RIGHT
Bourbon
'Honorine de Brabant'
makes bushy growth
with abundant pale pink
blooms delicately
marked with shades of
lilac – an attractive
variegated rose.

At the Isle of Bourbon the inhabitants generally inclose their land with hedges made of two sorts of roses, one of them Common China Rose and the other of the Red Four Seasons. Monsieur Perichon, a proprietor at St. Benoist, in the Isle, in planting one of these hedges, found amongst his young plants one very different from the others in its shoots and foliage. This induced him to plant it in his garden. It flowered the following year; and, as he anticipated, proved to be of quite a new race and differing much from the above two roses, *which at that time were the only sorts known in the island.*

M. Bréon went to Bourbon in 1817 as curator of the Botanical Garden and quickly propagated the rose, sending plants and seeds in 1822 to M. Jacques, the French Royal Gardener, who grew from seed 'Rosier de l'Île de Bourbon' (also known as 'Bourbon Jacques'), to be widely distributed in France and to reach England by 1828. Leading rosarian there, William Paul, was entranced with these new roses: 'The brilliancy and clearness of the colours, the large smooth petals of the flowers, their circular outline and beauty of the foliage have rendered them especial favourites.' He advised using the strongest to form handsome standards, the less vigorous, 'chaste and elegant', to train up pillars and poles, moderate growers to make dwarf standards, as well as others to be displayed as pot plants or, earlier, in the forcing house. He did not agree with planting them against walls.

However, I find this admirable because some of the Bourbons are weak-necked and respond well to support. For instance, 'Madame Pierre Oger' drooped her lovely, faintly blushing blooms in a border. I moved her to the house where, less reticent, she showed them to advantage very early (May 1987) and, cut back to promising eyes, equally well later, even to a third showing in October of that year. Also, I would defy anybody to suggest a better rose for wafting seductive fragrance through a window than 'Madame Isaac Pereire'; cerise, voluptuous, the very antithesis of 'Madame Pierre', she will 'climb' with support to 8 ft (2·4 m) and is ideal for a bungalow wall. Others are legitimate climbers and listed as such: cerise 'Zephirine Drouhin' is to be seen on houses the world over, in spite of a susceptibility to mildew, but I prefer 'Blairi No. 2', with an older look, its deep pink centre paling to the bloom's edge. It can be found covering an old fruit tree at the National Trust Rose Garden at Mottisfont in Hampshire. Climbing 'Souvenir de la Malmaison' has a wonderful scent with large quartered palest pink flowers – and, although the early blooms of this Bourbon are never good, it flowers over a long period.

An interesting note appears in the records of the Pennsylvania Horticulture Society for May 1832, when a Bourbon rose was shown and described as 'a hardy climbing variety, with large flowers similar in size and color to the Provence Rose, 8 feet [2·4 m] high, covered with flowers' and making a fine appearance. Buist was enthusiastic over Bourbons, saying that their perpetuity of bloom and hardiness 'filled up a chasm that had long been deplored by amateurs and cultivators in northern latitudes', and believed that soon, with the Remontants, they would be the only roses cultivated in the USA north of Virginia. He specifically mentioned importing in 1833 'Madame Desprez' (incidentally, a parent of 'Souvenir de la Malmaison') with Noisettes 'Aimée Vibert', 'Lamarque' and 'Jaune Desprez', with the comment, 'they will maintain their character for a quarter of a century to come and should be in every garden between this [Philadelphia] and Nachitoches'. In Toronto John Gray of the Grange Conservatories, listed in his 1846 *Catalogue of Green House Plants* (probably all available in pots) thirty-two Chinese Monthly or Bengal Roses, eight Noisettes, five Bourbons and fourteen Tea-Scented China Roses.

The last mentioned group had inherited astonishing shades from 'Hume's Blush' and 'Parks's Yellow': buff and salmon in 'Adam', the first Tea to be recognized in 1833; saffron, red-tinted buds opening to soft, buff-yellow in 'Safrano' (1837) and salmon with rosy pink in 'Souvenir d'un Ami' (1846).

Simplified geneology to show evolvement of main groups of garden roses.

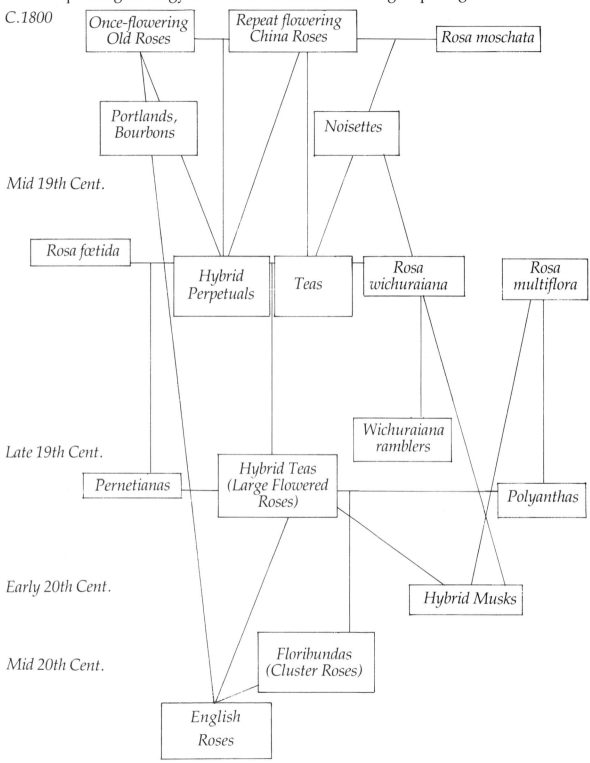

C.1800

Once-flowering Old Roses

Repeat flowering China Roses

Rosa moschata

Portlands, Bourbons

Noisettes

Mid 19th Cent.

Rosa fœtida

Hybrid Perpetuals

Teas

Rosa wichuraiana

Rosa multiflora

Wichuraiana ramblers

Late 19th Cent.

Pernetianas

Hybrid Teas (Large Flowered Roses)

Polyanthas

Early 20th Cent.

Hybrid Musks

Mid 20th Cent.

Floribundas (Cluster Roses)

English Roses

**Simple genealogical plan to show the influence of
China roses on subsequent groups.**

These were from France, where the majority were raised, but white 'Devoniensis' came from England in 1838 and the climbing form became universally popular. 'Safrano' proved immensely successful as a cut rose in Europe and was grown on the French Riviera for the winter trade. In the USA, Buist emphasized that winter protection was absolutely necessary for Teas in Pennsylvania and gave directions for constructing a 'substantial moveable frame to accommodate two hundred plants, whereby every lover of this celebrated rose in the eastern states can enjoy them in the greatest luxuriance from June to October'.

A report on gardens visited in Philadelphia appeared in the *Register of Pennsylvania* 12 February 1831 commenting on Mr Hart's 'very large Tea Rose withstanding last winter's frost, protected simply by a barrel' and also on his 'Greville Rose', in three years covering 200 sq. ft (18·58 sq. m) with a profusion of flowers of twelve to fifteen colours: 'a wonder and an ornament in any garden'. At the country seat of Mr L. Clapper, near Germantown, a gentleman 'distinguished for his generous encouragement of horticulture', it was noted that the Tea Rose flourished, 'cultivated in frames, it grows as large as any other rose bush in the garden'. Teas were seen mostly in conservatories in England, where their rather delicate constitution could be cherished and their scent appreciated. William Paul said of them, trained up to 12 ft (3·6 m) in one at Orleans House, Twickenham, 'nothing could be more appropriate, nothing more beautiful' and here their often hanging heads would have been seen to advantage from below. Grown in pots, they could be positioned outside in summer and moved to shelter in winter, as practised by those today who grow substantial Teas in containers.

However it is possible to plant them in a sheltered garden and they are increasingly appearing in catalogues. Peter Beales quotes 'Madame de Tartas', blush pink, as being one 'better outdoors than in' and I have some in my garden: 'Madame Wagram', a reddish-pink, 'Archiduc Joseph' of many shades and 'General Schablikine', coppery-red, all surviving cold winters with protection of bracken, as described for some Chinas. 'Perle des Jardins', a sulphurous yellow, seems hardy but hates bad weather. I thought 'Safrano' well established until two disastrous winters cut it to the ground. However in late June 1987, five good shoots with flower buds have shown me that it is wise never to abandon a rose for a year after such despoliation, but I never attempt to prune the Teas until April and then only lightly. I was quite proud of my little collection until I saw what they will do in gardens of California and Auckland, New Zealand, and appreciate that the majority do not show their best in northern Europe. The Victorians were right to cosset them under glass and they took prizes at the first Rose Shows, but could not compete in the garden with another class of Chinese descendants: the Hybrid Perpetuals.

To summarize the effect of the introduction of new roses arising from the China quartet, William Prince commented on the total change in public taste from the older roses to those 'with a long, successive display of floral beauties from the opening of spring until autumnal suspension of vegetation'. Roses from China had brought about a rapid revolution in the roses of the West.

CHAPTER 6

Discussion in Beijing and Finding Fa Tee

WITHOUT help from the dedicated son of a lady who devoted her life to improving roses in China, my experiences there would have hardly made a chapter. Having arranged to make the trip with the Garden History Society in the autumn of 1981 and as I usually divert in pursuit of roses, I tried to establish some rose contacts. Initially the Royal National Rose Society could give no lead and I was defeated, but at the Chelsea Flower Show in May 1981 Jill Bennell, on the Society's stand, told me that she had just heard from a gentleman in Tianjin who wished to join because of his late mother's great interest in roses.

I wrote at once and thus started a rewarding correspondence with Chen Di, a metallurgist who had

> inherited his mother's desire to make her country more beautiful and who edited a lot of material left behind by her, got into contact with people for exchanging new varieties and spent most of his spare time in translating books and articles on roses as well as doing research work ... the most sincere expression of a son in commemorating his deceased mother.

(I quote from the Preface to a Chinese book, *The Rose*, 1980, written by him and five others in memory of Jiang Entien.)

In his first leter to me Di said,

Jiang Entien, who did much to reinstate the rose in China, became known as 'Madame Rose', in her own garden.

> You have pointed out that Chinese roses have played a great part in the history of rose development around the world, but it is to be regretted that since two hundred years ago, China has been almost in an isolated condition from the outer world. The progress of Chinese rose growing almost stopped, few roses could have been exported. According to my mother's records, about 400 varieties of roses have been imported from abroad in the past 50 years, which is important for China, but not so important for the rest of the world, I'm afraid. I think the really important thing is: if we can find some roses in China which are unknown to the world. China is a large country many places are still not explored. I have read a piece of news in *People's Daily* (a major Chinese paper, the date was 27 May 1981) which said 630 hectares of wild roses have just been discovered in Xin Jiang (a Province in the North-West of China). Perhaps there are still some valuable species growing in our land and they can help us to improve the roses we already have. I think it is the common interest of both you and me.

This encouraging reply was followed by more letters, telling me about Jiang Entien. In the 1950s, she had taken over more than 300 varieties of rare roses from abroad and other plants of China from an aged overseas Chinese rose lover when he died. She cultivated them in her own garden and in 1958 after the completion of the Great Hall of the People she accepted the invitation of the Beijing municipal authorities to help design flowerbeds around the Hall, where she and her husband planted all their roses. 'On National Day, 1 October 1959, the roses in front of the Hall came into bloom beautifully; all foreign and domestic guests lingered around the flowerbeds and could not tear themselves away' (from an article by Chen Di, translated by his brother-in-law, Shen Zongyuang).

Next she became adviser to the Gardening and Afforestation Bureau and, working with an expert gardener, Lui Haoqin, she created the rose garden in the Temple of Heaven Park, Beijing, living there and experimenting with propagation and cultivation, working on classification and naming, exchanging seeds and information with other rosarians in the country. By 1965 there were more than 600 indigenous and overseas varieties in the garden and Jiang Entien had become known as 'Madame Rose'. Sadly, she died in 1975 before she was able to make another garden of roses for the Xiang Shan (Fragrant Mountain) Botanical Institute in Beijing.

In October 1981 our delayed arrival caused Chen Di to wait seven hours at Beijing Airport. He was anxious to tell me that he had organized a meeting early the following day and an interview for television with the Beijing Scientific Education Film Studio, for which I had to do some quick thinking.

The Summer Palace was first on the Society's schedule for next morning, but this had to be forfeited for roses and the coach dropped me and my friend Joy Lee at the zoo, where we were met by Di. For the meeting he had assembled Professor Chen Junyu, in charge of Landscape Gardening, Beijing College of Forestry, Mrs Zhu Xiuzhen, President of the Beijing Rose Society, Mr Chang Qing of the Institute of Contemporary International Relations, film director Ms Sandra Setu, daughter of Mr Setu Huimin, a pioneer in Chinese film industry and more recently Deputy Minister of Culture, Mr Chen Yu Hua, lecturer at the Beijing Institute of Technology, a celebrated artist, and Mr Xie Feng, a leading photographer. Over tea we discussed the cut roses and foliage brought by the Professor. He told us that there are more than sixty species of roses in China and of these fifteen are used in modern rose breeding. The small crimson-flowered *R. chinensis* 'Semperflorens' he thought to be synonymous with 'Slater's Crimson China' and bloom on 'Viridiflora' was a much stronger green than any I had seen before. Pieces of *R. xanthina*, *R. xanthina spontanea* and *R. primula* had long since lost their flowers, but I did find foliage of the 'Moutan' or 'Peony Rose' interesting – large and coarse

Illustration from *The Rose*, 1980, a book compiled in appreciation of the work of Jiang Entien by her son and others.

9月初～9月中	10月	11月下旬～12月初	3月～4月	5月中旬
基部多头嵌芽接	修剪部分枝梢	切顶裸根冷藏	花坛定植	形成月季园

compared with the rest and reminiscent of some of our Hybrid Perpetuals. The Professor said this was a cultivar from Shandung Province in north China, quite old and blooming 'one and a half times a year', with colours ranging from white and pink to purple. It is also sometimes known as the 'Shandung Rose'. He was, he said, doing much research on hybridization and was anxious to discover more about the original garden cultivars. Areas famed for them are Yen Lin, Honan Province; Ye Xian, Shandong Province; Xian, Shanxi Province, and Chengdu, Sichuan Province. I was also told about old rose publications, learning that records of roses go way back to the Han Dynasty (206 BC–AD 221), over a thousand years ago, and that there is a detailed account in the Sung Dynasty (960–1276), in which forty-one varieties in the gardens of Loyang are listed. All have very beautiful names and full descriptions of their colour, fragrance and foliage.

During the television recording I stressed how much the West owes to China; without Chinese roses, we would have only a limited display of bloom. Another point I mentioned in favour of using Chinese garden roses in breeding was that they are comparatively disease-resistant. I explained about the progeny of the Four Stud Chinas and emphasized that we use many Chinese species in hybridization. I was asked about the old roses of the West and gathered that the Chinese would like to see more of them. Incidentally, 'Rosamundi' is the only one to appear among some sixty close-ups in colour of modern roses in the book written in memory of Jiang Entien where it is captioned as 'Versicolor'.

We were taken for our first lunch in China to a busy restaurant specializing in food from Guangzhou in the South. Rose discussion continued throughout the meal and later back at the zoo, when I was presented with one of Chen Yu Hua's lovely rose paintings, inscribed with a poem written by Sun Dong Po of the Sung Dynasty. Later I asked Di for a translation and he sent one by Professor Ye Junjian, a famous contemporary writer, the first two lines of which read as follows:

Flowers generally cannot keep their rose hues more than ten days,
But this one remains fresh all the time as though in spring breeze.

I was very moved by this charming gesture and generous reception on my arrival in China.

The following day Di had arranged for the Society to visit the Park of Temple of Heaven Rose Garden and he was waiting to greet us with Lui Haoqin and Mr Xu Zhichang, horticulturist at the Garden and Professor Wang Juyuan of the Bureau of Parks Administration. The majority of the modern roses had been cut back two months previously in order to be at their best again for the national holiday in about ten days' time.

However, I was excited to find at the far end of the garden two long borders of flowering Chinese cultivars, most of them unknown to me. I asked for English names and was told a pale pink single translated as 'Village of Apricot Blossom'; a small clustered pink, 'In Memory of Martia' and a fully double 'Souzhou Pink', all with typical red-tinged China foliage. We were taken to the adjoining rose nursery to see a vast collection of roses in grey clay pots, grown from cuttings. These, just 2 in (5 cm) long, are taken from pruned stems after

FAR LEFT
My valued picture from
China by Chen Yu Hua,
owner of rose nurseries
in Beijing and Shenzhen.

The 'Moutan' or 'Paeony
Rose' from Shandung in
North China, produces
blooms up to 5 inches
across in Hampshire.

BELOW
Small red
R. semperflorens type of
rose seen growing widely
throughout North China,
flowers continuously
over a long period.

Taking notes of China cultivars in Park of Heaven Temple Rose Garden, Beijing from Professor Wang Jujuan, with Chen Di, right and Liu Haoqin, left.

blooming in June or July and are then planted in one part sand and two parts soil, with fertilizer added. They are kept completely shaded for the first ten days and then, with gradually increased sunlight, rooting starts after twenty days, when they must still be shielded from the midday sun.

There were in the nursery quantities of the curious green 'Viridiflora' and examples of bonsai roses, as well as many lovely Teas of delicate shades. However, I was told that bestsellers in 1981 were 'Peace', 'Chicago Peace' and 'Super Star'; large-bloomed, long-flowering roses descended from the Chinas of 200 years ago.

We journeyed south via Nanjing, Wuxi and Suzhou, spending some time in the famous old gardens, finding roses in colourful containers placed against sombre backgrounds and species, planted carefully for spring display, as in the Zhan Yuan, Nanjing, a garden made some 600 years ago, where *R. banksiae* cascades down a 'fairy peak' of ancient rocks. We left this city by the South Gate in the massive wall and were surprised to find a rose nursery tucked away within the ramparts, well insulated from excessive heat or cold.

In the Li Yuan, Suzhou, *R. chinensis* 'Semperflorens' was used quite widely; vivid crimson flowers well displayed against greys and greens of stone and conifer. The single pink Chinese cultivar, seen in the Temple of Heaven garden, seemed the rose most widely grown in public places; for instance, around the Tai Lake at Wuxi and in borders beside a silk factory at Suzhou, where even the station was embellished with roses around buffers. Here, a town often known as the Venice of China for its many canals, a square might be bare one evening save for a few chalk marks on the paving and next morning would be transformed with roses in dramatic display, pots stacked tier upon tier. A bicycle might become a mobile rose tableau. Potted blooms hung on every part, piled in a huge basket in front and a small trailer behind, they were transported most precariously.

Sir John Keswick had told me that Hangzhou was renowned for rose display and he had obtained many for them, but unfortunately the rain poured incessantly during our time there and we were unable to enjoy the plantings around the lake. It was difficult to find roses in Shanghai, but I noticed some striking yellow blooms on the balcony of a monastery, their pots placed prominently for all to see. We diverted from gardens to Kweilin; I was not expecting to detect roses in that dramatic mountain landscape, but I discovered *R. multiflora*, growing wild and covered with hips, when exploring the limestone hill behind the hotel early one morning.

Next we were in Guangzhou and I was much looking forward to meeting another contact, arranged by Chen Di before I left England, from whom I had received a courteous letter: '. . . the climate here is sub-tropical, not adapted for roses; there are only a few common ones which we have just introduced to make a trial. However, the cultivation of roses is my predilection and I hope we can meet to talk over Chinese roses'. Professor Chen Fenghuai, an energetic octogenarian of the South China Institute of Botany, had been a friend of Di's parents and he spared time to charm us with an account of meetings with Frank Kingdon Ward (the collector who made several expeditions to China between 1911 and 1939) and of his own specialist work with lily and primula. He told us of his time at the Edinburgh Botanic Garden and also at Kew and then described the Guangzhou Garden, created on very much the same lines, preparing us for an extensive tour. This, in spite of trying humid heat, was most rewarding, especially to see so many species of bamboo and to learn of their many and varied uses.

The Professor gave me a list of roses grown in the garden in 1959, twenty-one in all, including *R. centifolia* and *R. c. var. muscosa*. The rest were species and the Professor told me he was particularly interested in their use in hybridization in the West and asked for some information about our modern roses bred from the wild ones of China. Later I sent him a comprehensive list and included our much cherished 'Wedding Day' from *R. sinowilsonii*; 'Mermaid' from *R. bracteata*; 'Marguerite Hilling' from *R. moyesii*; 'Lykke-fund' from *R. helenae* in Denmark; 'Cerise Bouquet' from *R. multibracteata* in Germany; 'Silver Moon' from *R. laevigata* in America; and 'Lorraine Lee' from *R. gigantea* in Australia. In his reply Professor Chen said, '*R. roxburgii* and *R. laevigata* contain rich Vitamin C. The former, we old Chinese physicians used as a herb for treating children.' In another letter for the New Year, he stressed, 'Let us all understand that English and Chinese worked together on plant introductions two hundred years ago. The collaboration of this work will, I think, be continued successfully now . . .'

I had always hoped to trace the site of the Fa Tee Gardens and mentioned this to the Professor. He knew nothing about them, but thought a horticultural commune working on the south-west side of the city might be worth a visit. I knew that this was the area of the old nursery gardens and so suggested the commune as an alternative to the tour of Guangzhou on our itinerary. The party agreed to split and I think the majority opted out of the city for what proved to be a rather hazardous journey. The driver was sceptical of finding the way, the traffic was solid as we approached the Peace River crossing, a thunderstorm caused a deluge and, out in the country, we had to abandon the coach and wade through mud while it negotiated a rickety bridge. I began to feel that perhaps we should give up, but the sun came out and we found the commune interesting, especially in its propagation methods. The only roses I could find were a vast quantity of *R. chinensis* 'Semperflorens' in various stages of growth, ranged in the usual grey pots. Through the guide, I asked the commune leader whether he knew of any old nurseries in the area and he at once replied that a brigade worked in one nearby and that it would be possible to visit it. When the coach stopped outside a walled garden, I learned that the inscription over the gateway meant 'Fa Tee'.

Inside the little garden, now filled with bonsai, I asked an old gardener if roses were grown there now. Shaking his head he said no, but added, 'Many, many years ago, beautiful roses were grown here.' The layout was very much like Robert Fortune's description of the East India Company's garden: it was small and walled, with a path around the perimeter and trees in the middle, including an old frangipani. I found myself thinking back to the days when traders had come here to buy plants, Livingstone to assess the soil and Reeves to select promising rosebuds to open for his skilled artists. It was just possible they all had been, if not there, then to a similar garden nearby. This was undoubtedly one of my best moments in China, as I reported to Professor Chen, who has since been to see it himself.

But all was entirely due to Di Chen, as he is now known in the USA. Soon after our meeting in China, he left to study there and two years later was joined by his wife, Jie and Rosemary, as I named their child, my adopted grand-daughter. I stayed with them when in California and was glad to learn that Di had organized shipments from Jackson & Perkins, leading rosegrowers in Oregon, for the well-known and generous C. B. Sung and his wife, Beulah, who have done much to promote roses in China.

I have since heard that Chen Yu Hua, the artist, has extended his love of flowers by establishing first, the Bei Fang Rose Garden in Beijing and secondly, a large nursery in the Shenzhen Special Economic Zone in order to supply nearby Hong Kong throughout the year and northern Chinese cities during the winter months. He told me recently that he is now obtaining roses from England, France, Holland and Japan to establish a substantial flow from West to East. I asked him if there was any old rose he favours. He replied,

It is not easy to say which rose I particularly love as there are so many wonderful varieties. But I'd like to name *Rosa rugosa* as my choice. It is a native of China and for many centuries its strongly perfumed flower has been used as a very popular flavouring in making all kinds of cakes, sweets and other delicacies. The flower is also used in black tea and wine. Today *Rosa rugosa* is still widely grown in many places in China, not for decorative purposes but for its economic value. Although I don't grow this rose in my nursery, I think it is an important rose in China and deserves admiration.

I was very gratified to hear that he would like my book to be available to Chinese readers.

Di has been to see me twice in Hampshire, his work as a steel consultant now bringing him to England. First we went to Wisley, where he was intrigued to see roses trained on ropes. The next visit took in the house of his favourite English author, Jane Austen, at Chawton, Hampshire, where roses she would have known have been planted in the garden and include 'Old Blush China'. I value very much my friendship with the son of 'Madame Rose' who stresses the importance of international rose relations:

RIGHT
'Tipsy Imperial Concubine', brought to me by Professor Ye Junjian from China, flowers well in early summer and autumn.

The development and progress of the different cultures in the world are usually made through intercourse and exchange. It is the same with roses. If there had not been hybridization and cultivation in Europe, we would not have been able to enjoy so many varieties of exceptionally wonderful roses. Of course, we are glad to know that Chinese roses have made some contribution to the development of roses in the world.

The exchange is operating: in 1982 cuttings of three varieties were brought over to me by Professor Ye Junjian and his wife, another rose enthusiast and member of the Beijing Rose Society. These were grown on by Peter Beales at Attleborough and Jim Russell at Castle Howard; both have sent roses back to China. Now I have this trio established in my own garden: a small-flowered unidentified crimson, flowering from May to the first hard frosts, the 'Moutan Rose', flowering one and a half times, as I was told at the zoo meeting and looking like a full loose-petalled peony, and a Tea Rose with the unlikely name 'Tipsy Imperial Concubine', as translated from the Chinese. This blush–cream beauty, opening from buds touched with carmine, produces alluring summer and autumn blooms. I also have two seedlings, grown from hips collected by Heather on one of her many photographic expeditions to China, one upright and bushy, the other more lax and spreading and I look forward to some blooms next year. With 'Old Blush China', 'Parks's Yellow', 'Fortune's Yellow' and representatives of most Chinese descendants, I am reminded of Fa Tee and my Chinese friends whenever I am working on my borders, and indoors Chen Yu Hua's roses will never fade.

Part III

VICTORIAN BOUNTY TO THE ANTIPODES

Roses which are chosen for their more perfect
beauty, like the fairest maidens at some public fête

S. REYNOLDS HOLE, *Book About Roses* (1869)

'*Général Jacqueminot*'

CHAPTER 7

Roses for Exhibition

By 1837, when Victoria came to the throne, a great number of new roses with varying qualities were available. Breeders, using the best of them, produced a new class. This was to be known as Hybrid Perpetual, although these roses were in no way perpetual and the French name of Hybride Remontant was the more correct; they flowered in summer and the majority made a lesser showing in the autumn. Among the earliest were 'La Reine' and 'Baronne Prévost', introduced by Laffay and Desprez in 1842, roses to herald the class, to be acclaimed universally and to dominate rose growing for the next forty years. The two leading rosarians in England at this time were William Paul and Thomas Rivers. Both had extensive nurseries: Paul's was founded in 1806 at Cheshunt and left to his brother George in 1860 when he moved to Waltham Cross, and Rivers

Thomas Rivers
(1789–1877), taken from a
miniature through the
courtesy of his family at
Sawbridgeworth.

inherited Sawbridgeworth, originally founded by his grandfather in 1727 and well known for its fruit, but under him to become a significant rose establishment also. Both wrote books running into many editions: Paul's classic *The Rose Garden*, with beautiful coloured plates in the first, ninth and tenth, was justly extolled and Rivers's *The Rose Amateur's Guide*, a smaller, essentially practical handbook, was followed by countless readers.

Both bred roses; the Paul or Rivers prefix was to be found in every catalogue, and they were also deeply involved with the promotion of Hybrid Perpetuals. I have looked more closely into Rivers through the courtesy of one of his descendants, who allowed me to study his own collection of books and catalogues at Sawbridgeworth. Rivers's catalogue sowed the seed of this story of worldwide roses, so I am here choosing him as an example of an industrious Victorian who, as well as undertaking a prodigious amount of practical work in his nursery, also had time to visit contemporaries in Europe, entertain others from abroad and maintain a wide and varied correspondence. He seemed to have some rapport with Laffay; the French grower's early deep red Hybrid Perpetual was named 'Rivers' and this was advocated by Buist in the USA: 'During the whole season it produces its extremely large flowers in clusters of brilliant crimson inclining to scarlet; it is very fragrant and a great favourite, but quite scarce.' Both Laffay and Rivers demonstrated a fondness for Moss Roses; every one from France was claimed to be represented at Sawbridgeworth and a few were consistently maintained in the catalogue, although the number of old summer-flowering roses fell from 200 in 1840 to eighteen in 1872.

Of the newcomers about to dominate the scene, Rivers said, 'Certainly a more beautiful and interesting class of roses does not exist; their flowers are large, very double, most fragrant and produced until the end of October ... perfectly hardy and will grow well in any climate in Great Britain however far north.' This was endorsed half a century on when the Rev A. Foster Melliar in *The Book of the Rose* (London, 1905) went as far as to say,

> The Hybrid Perpetual is the Rose of England, for not only are the best crimsons and reds with which a rose is generally associated to be found in this class, but also it is undoubtedly better grown in the British Isles than anywhere else. It has been said of our climate that it has no weather, but only samples: this exactly suits the Hybrid Perpetuals, which like a cool, damp one and long continued 'weather' of any sort will prevent them from coming to perfection.

Hybrid Perpetuals available today vary considerably in appearance and behaviour: blooms may be cupped, flat, high-centred, quartered or rosette. Some make compact bushes, 'Eliza Boelle' and 'American Beauty' for instance; others, like 'Paul Ricault' and 'Georg Arends', grow tall, while 'Prince Camille de Rohan' is more lax. On the whole, foliage is rather coarse, balancing often heavy blooms. Rivers' *Descriptive Catalogue* of 1872–3 grouped the wide selection of colours under headings ranging from bright crimson and scarlet, carmine, rose-coloured and pink, blush and flesh, to white. Among the darkest 'Souvenir d'Alphonse Lavallée' is, I think, one of the best – it has the depth of 'Tuscany' in purple-crimson velvety blooms although rather recalcitrant and better tethered. Neater is 'Enfant de France', a full, clear pink, and of the whites I prefer 'Gloire Lyonnaise' of exemplary deportment. Perhaps 'Reine des Violettes' is one of the loveliest, with lilac, violet and purple shadings, and among variegated Hybrid Perpetuals, both 'Baron Girod de L'Ain' and 'Roger Lambelin' have deep crimson fluted petals edged with white.

The Sawbridgeworth catalogue drew attention to their suitability as pillar roses, trained to an 8 ft (2·4 m) iron stake, and suggested displaying 'Baronne Prévost', 'Jules Margottin' and 'Lord Raglan' in this way. J. C. Loudon had earlier described how roses were planted in groups on lawn or gravel

> either with common box or other edgings or with edgings or wire, in imitation of basketwork. They are called baskets of roses, the ground enclosed in the basket margin is made convex, so as to present a greater surface to the eye and increase the illusion; the shoots of the stronger sorts are layered or kept down by pegs till they strike root into the ground . . . the whole surface of the basket becomes in two or three years covered with rosebuds and leaves of one or various sorts.
>
> *An Encyclopaedia of Gardening*, revised edition (1835)

Here, Loudon was suggesting Provins or Moss Roses, but Hybrid Perpetuals responded particularly well to manipulation and were often displayed in this way. I have been able to grow some of them by attaching their robust stems to strong tent pegs in order to obtain low floriferous arches of bloom in a position where their normal tall growth could not be accommodated.

I think Thomas Rivers inclined towards the deep reds. He maintained that one was the spark to kindle his fire of rose enthusiasm: a chance discovery in a batch of China seedlings in his nursery 'eclipsed all dark roses known' and he named it 'George IV' (1820). This was to enrapture Buist on a visit to Sawbridgeworth from Philadelphia and for him it became a good seller in the USA. Three Canadian nurseries extolled 'George IV' in their catalogues over twenty years in the middle of the century, as 'large and fine', 'deep velvet crimson' and 'very double'.

Rivers himself played a part in promoting one of two famous red Victorian Hybrid Perpetuals: he thought 'Géant des Batailles' (1846) 'the most bright and brilliant of all roses', and in the autumn of 1848 dispersed 8,000 standards and dwarfs all over the country. In Australia the Brunning nursery at Melbourne priced the 'Géant' at 10s 6d (with 'Cloth of Gold' the most expensive in the 1855 catalogue), claiming it to be the finest rose ever grown. It was still listed in 1898 as 'a very old variety and very useful in the bud for bouquets, retained for being the first imported hybrid perpetual rose propagated in the colony [Victoria] by our late Mr. B. senior'.

The second, 'Général Jacqueminot', was introduced in 1853 and described ten years later by David Hay of Auckland as 'most brilliant, crimson, scarlet, even surpassing Géant des Batailles, the best in this class'. Eighteen years later, Henderson of New York, emphasized, 'This is now the most fashionable of all roses, or winter flowers' and thought that probably 200,000 sq. ft (18,580 sq. m) of greenhouses were devoted exclusively to its growth in the vicinity of New York for the purpose of forcing it. Still the praise continued: B. A. Elliott & Co., Plantsmen of Pittsburgh had 'never had better success with Hybrid Perpetuals than in last summer and autumn; one bed of

Jacqueminots containing a hundred plants gave us quantities of bloom daily from June to September' (*A Few Flowers Worthy of General Culture*, Pittsburgh, 1899). Finally, forty years after introduction, T. B. Jenkins added his applause:

> In 1853 France gave us Général Jacqueminot, leader of the Hybrid Perpetuals; the grand, dark crimson rose, so sturdy in growth, rich in bloom and powerful in colour. The great half grown crimson buds have slept on the bosom of every belle since that day and they have been sold by the hundred for as many dollars to New York dealers and were retailed, no doubt, for twice that sum. A few days before one Christmas the only Jacqueminot buds to be found in the city were sold for $15 each or eight times their weight in gold.
>
> *Roses and Rose Culture*, Rochester, N.Y. (1892)

The 'Général' was, without any doubt, an eminent Victorian.

We gain a little insight into the Sawbridgeworth Nursery from an account by American visitors, which I discovered in volume V p. 181 of *The Horticulturist and Journal of Rural Art and Rural Tastes* (July–September, 1850), a publication that a few years earlier had quoted Rivers 'as yet the best author on the rose' and 'head of the English growers of the Rose'. The report stated:

Rivers advocated 'Reine des Violettes' as a spectacular pillar rose; but its wonderful purple and violet shades are rarely reproduced accurately.

> We lingered nearly two days with Mr. Rivers who, we must be allowed to say, is not only a horticulturist, but a thoroughly agreeable and cultivated man . . . [his] establishment is famous on both sides of the Atlantic for its collection of roses. Here we saw acres of the finest varieties propagated and ready for sale. Although the rose season was past, yet the perpetuals were gay with the finest flowers. The two sorts which particularly attracted our attention were 'Géant des Batailles' and 'Standard of Marengo', both a rich, deep crimson wh. may be described as a fiery red.

Comment continued on thousands of the Manetti stock and use of Célène as another, on the 'extensive range of new pits with sunken beds or borders, under which warm pipes circulate so as to communicate a genial bottom heat . . . a continual system of propagation at all seasons' and on Rivers's own garden at Bonks Hill, 'prettily dotted with rare weeping trees and standard perpetual roses'. When I was there in 1980, I was pleased to see a dark Moss Rose growing against the house, representing one of his favourite kinds and colour.

In his *Guide* Rivers encouraged the amateur to experiment with breeding, exhorting him to try for a 'mossy Bourbon' or 'yellow Ayrshire' and to practise somewhat adventurous budding. He exclaimed light-heartedly, 'Did I not consider myself at 20 the most dextrous and rapid budder of roses that ever lived or was likely to live?' when describing his part in camouflaging an ugly bridge for a friend at Guildford. He first planted varieties of *R. sempervirens* and then decorated them by budding with Hybrid Perpetuals. Eleven months later 'amid the pale climbing roses shone forth large clusters' of the Géant, Général Jacqueminot, Jules Margottin, Colonel de Rougemont and others, to make a positive fairy avenue. He advised those wishing for something quite recherché in rose trees to bud 'Félicité Perpétue' on short old Dog Rose stock and, left unpruned, it would eventually provide a perfect dome. He mentioned the skill of his son, Thomas Francis, with double working for the beautiful Tea Rose 'Maréchal Niel', budding it on 'Gloire de Dijon', originally budded on Manetti stock, a method generally adopted with outstanding results.

Charles Darwin appreciated this rosarian's expertise, as is shown in a batch of letters from the scientist in the early 1870s. At that time he was writing a book on the variation of animals and plants under domestication and asked for 'one little piece of information which it is more likely that you could give me than any man in the world ... I am collecting all accounts of what some call sports, that is, of which I shall call "bud variations", i.e. a moss rose suddenly opening on a provence, a nectarine on a peach etc ...' Reply was prompt and Darwin said he had never received a kinder letter and added, 'For years I have read with interest every scrap which you have written in periodicals and abstracted in MS from your book on Roses.' A later letter commented, 'The case of Baronne Prévost with its different shoots, foliage, spikes and flowers will be grand to quote.'

Around the middle of the century Rivers recognized a new trend: horticultural societies were offering prizes for roses in pots, Teas of greenhouse culture being the obvious choice. However, in the eleventh edition of *The Rose Amateur's Guide*, he describes how hardy varieties can thus be grown to provide magnificent plants, listing two dozen Hybrid Perpetuals, including 'Madame Rivers', an unusual blush from Guillot of Lyon, described by Paul as having a delicate complexion. One difficulty with growing these pot roses in the open for exhibition purposes was timing their perfection. Rivers suggested they could be forced by a week in the greenhouse or, 'to retard them, the method employed by the courtier, in the days of Elizabeth, to save his cherries for his queen, may be essayed, viz. stretch a piece of canvas on hoops over the plants and keep it constantly wet by sprinkling it with water'.

As the Victorian roses improved with emphasis on the most spectacular blooms, competition became widespread, production geared to exhibition. Dean Reynolds Hole (President of the National Rose Society, 1877–1904) devotes a third of his *Book about Roses* (1869) on how best to show them and was well qualified in this respect. He had conceived the idea of the First National Rose Show and, helped by Paul, Rivers and Charles Turner, 'prince of florists', it was staged in London on 1 July 1858. The occasion was a resounding success, rose nurseries pouring their treasures into St James's Hall, as the Dean quoted from Dr Lindley's report in *The Gardeners' Chronicle*.

In his book he glowingly paid tribute to 'our Commander-in-Chief – that veteran hero, Rivers of Sawbridgeworth, who still issues in his Guide to Amateurs those orders and wise counsels which lead to victory'. They would almost certainly have been followed by the artisan rose growers of Nottingham from whom the Dean received a letter asking him to 'assist in a judicial capacity' at an exhibition of roses on Easter Monday. Now at that time he had not a single rose out, but his scepticism was soon dispelled when he found, in the upstairs room of an inn, a quite wondrous display of bloom. He writes of the best examples he had ever seen of 'Maréchal Niel' (one of his favourite roses), 'Madame Margottin' and 'Alphonse Karr', displayed that spring in ginger-beer bottles, and of how, afterwards, he was taken to allotments and

OVERLEAF TOP
An unusual Hybrid Perpetual, Baron Girod de l'Ain, sport of 'Eugène Furst', appeared at the beginning of this century; seen here at Sissinghurst.

OVERLEAF BOTTOM
'Gloire Lyonnaise', upstanding Hybrid Perpetual from France, 1885, 'cannot fail to please the most fastidious'. (Henderson of New York, 1888).

OVERLEAF RIGHT
Offspring of *R. multiflora* and a yellow Tea Rose, 'Perle d'Or', a Polyantha with perfect buds, was also called 'The Buttonhole Rose'.

learned that beds had been bereft of blankets in order to insulate tiny greenhouses and protect precious Noisettes, Teas and Hybrid Perpetuals from frost. This evoked extravagant summing up from the judge: 'They ought to be presented with a golden warming-pan, set with brilliants and filled with fifty-pound Bank of England notes.'

Current gardening periodicals emphasized the effect of inclement weather upon roses during the summer of 1888. *The Garden* anticipated old and species roses flowering in August and, reporting on a visit to Waltham Cross, found the Paul Tea Roses, particularly 'Madame de Watteville', badly affected by the capricious season. 'Devoniensis' ranked with the best in such conditions and a buxom standard of 'Perle des Jardins' was noticed in the garden.

At the end of July, this journal described the new exhibition roses; those from Henry Bennett of Shepperton being the most successful, although 'Her Majesty', splendid earlier in the year, had suffered latterly. 'Viscountess Folkestone' had proved a light-coloured rose to 'rise superior to dripping skies and absence of sunshine' and 'Princess Beatrice', a long-lasting yellow-orange Tea, had proved popular with the florists. However, 'Mrs. John Laing' had appeared 'in all directions as bright and as fresh as possible, in spite of the interminable succession of wet days'. A decade later, Henderson of New York still believed this to be Bennett's best rose, proving perfectly hardy in the northern states.

R. polyantha grandiflora illustrated in *The Journal of Horticulture*, Vol. XVI, 1888, gained a first class certificate when smaller roses were becoming popular.

Two roses from abroad were in *The Garden*'s list: 'The Bride', sport of 'Catherine Mermet' from the USA and likened to the 'tint of pale yellow, typical of a good lemon water ice'. 'Madame Henri Pereire', a crimson Hybrid Perpetual exhibited by Paul, was the only French rose to appear consistently. The appraisal concluded that although the French Tea novelties were superior on account of a kinder climate, their Hybrid Perpetuals were in the minority and England was raising the better roses.

Show entries fell drastically and in August *The Gardeners' Chronicle* reported that of the 543 entries at the National Rose Society Show, only 306 had been staged. Lighter coloured roses were worse affected: a class for twelve blooms of 'Her Majesty' was reduced from ten to one exhibit and 'Lady Mary Fitzwilliam' fell from fifteen to three. These were recent leading Hybrid Perpetuals and some of the dark old favourites like 'General Jack' (as it was affectionately called by many), 'Charles Lefèbvre' and 'Prince Arthur' came to the fore.

Two correspondents wrote to Loudon's *The Journal of Horticulture* in September; one pointing out that the only summer weather, ten days in August, had caused slow-openers, like 'La Boule d'Or', to come out completely in two to three days. The other had collected eels instead of roses from his garden. The following month, October, the same publication pointed out that Paul's vigorous crimson Hybrid Perpetual 'Duke of Edinburgh' had been admirably suited to the season and 'Gloire de Dijon' was proving to be one of the finest autumn roses in existence. 'Maréchal Niel' and 'William Allen Richardson' gained commendation in the garden of Mr Mawley, at that time joint Secretary, with the Rev H. H. d'Ombrian, of the National Rose Society.

Double dwarf Polyanthas had originated in France from a low-growing Multiflora and a China Hybrid; 'Paquerette' being the first in 1875. Later varieties like 'Perle d'Or' and 'Cécile Brunner' were becoming increasingly popular and George Paul thought their improvement with perpetual larger flowers might result in a hardy race of Hybrid Teas. Here was foresight because eventually they led to the all-important Floribundas, or Cluster Roses.

Paul had included this observation at the National Rose Conference in his paper 'Roses Since 1860', when he summarized the situation some thirty years on. In 1857, fifty-four Hybrid Perpetuals had won first prizes and among them only 'Général Jacqueminot' remained. However, all the Ten Teas then exhibited still persisted, so more progress had been made with the former. From 1859 to 1879 there was a surge in Hybrid Perpetuals and by 1889 Teas had trebled in number since the 1860s, though the class of Hybrid Teas had made no real advance. On the other hand, Rugosas were progressing with the introduction of 'Madame George Bruant' (1887), while other new roses of note were Mosses, 'Blanche Moreau' and 'Little Gem'; Hybrid Bourbon, 'Madame Isaac Pereire' and Noisettes, 'William A. Richardson' and 'L'Idéale'.

There was as yet no indication that the emphasis on roses for exhibition was soon to be redirected, but before pursuing that course, a backward look must be taken to see how Victorian roses were being grown elsewhere, whither my attention was directed by a note in the Sawbridgeworth catalogue: 'Roses and Forest Trees can now be sent to the most distant Colonies without hazard and should be shipped for New Zealand and Australia in December.'

CHAPTER 8

Australian Roses Established

As there are no roses indigenous to the southern hemisphere, all had to be introduced to Australia, taken by early settlers and treasured in faraway gardens. For a thorough account of early horticultural activity, I would refer readers to *Cherish the Earth* by Beatrice Bligh (Sydney, 1973), where roses are frequently mentioned. Here, I shall only include on the historic side a few early private and botanic garden collections, information gleaned from nursery catalogues and a later noteworthy Australian rose breeder. My travel experiences are limited to Victoria and South Australia, but I hope that they will give some indication of the serious revival of interest in Australia's early roses today.

'Unless you could see them you would not believe how beautiful the roses are here,' was the ecstatic comment from Georgiana Lowe, wife of Robert, Viscount Sherbrooke who lived at Bronte House, Sydney in the 1840s. She had been visiting Elizabeth Bay House, home of Alexander Macleay, a careful recorder of his garden plantings from 1830 and his list of thirty-four roses is impressive in diversity. It consists of five Gallica, four Alba, six Damask, six Centifolia, one Moss, two China ('Hume's Blush' and 'Parks's Yellow'), three Noisette and seven species. A descriptive leaflet of this property today indicates that some were imported direct from China and also that seed was obtained from Robert Scott's nursery in England. I have asked John Harvey about this and he knows of no one else of that name than John Scott who took over a nursery at Merriott in Somerset in 1848 so I have been unable to look further into that source.

Alexander Macleay also obtained roses from William Macarthur at Camden Park, whose parents, John and Elizabeth, came to Australia and grew roses at their first home, Elizabeth Farm, built at Granville in 1793. A great number of plants were introduced into the colony by John Macarthur when he returned a second time in 1817 and records show that 'roses and jessamines' were included for use in perfume. In 1848 Elizabeth wrote to her son, Edward, in Ireland:

> The China rose introduced into the colony by your dear father is now blooming into [a] blaze of beauty around the garden fences and in various places now almost in every cottage . . . yielding flowers more or less throughout the year. We have a variety of other Roses, sweet-scented and beautiful in their season, but not so enduring.

In 1825 Edward had sent twenty roses to his brother, William, obviously an enthusiastic rosarian because by 1843 a *Catalogue of Plants cultivated at Camden* named twenty-six, with 'many others' mentioned. Two years later this was increased to forty-three, including varieties like 'Queen of the Prairies', 'Boule de Nanteuil' and 'Jaune Desprez'. Under the Historic Houses Trust of New South Wales, Elizabeth Farm has now been opened as an historic house museum and the garden is restored and planted with the 'Old Blush China' and other old summer-flowering roses cherished by Elizabeth Macarthur. I am grateful to its curator, Susan Hunt, for helping with information here.

'*A Catalogue of Plants* introduced into South Australia by George Stevenson Esq. and grown at Melbourne Cottage, North Adelaide, compiled by George McEwin' and dated 1843 lists six roses: 'Provence, double moss, double white moss, sweetbriar, officinal and Scotch'. It is interesting to see listed under hardy, ornamental climbing shrubs, a further seven: three multiflora (many-flowered, light purple and white) as well as a China and three China forms (dark double purple, Edwards's and a large double centifolia). Reeves had in his collection of drawings painted by the Chinese a purple double rose and a large pink double centifolia, which seem exactly to tie up with descriptions given here.

By 1857 the *Catalogue of Plants* in the Government Botanic Garden, Sydney, included a substantial list of roses, giving the country of origin for seventeen species. Although eighty-six named garden varieties are in alphabetical order with no classification, it proves a most comprehensive collection representing all the old summer flowerers as well as nineteenth-century roses: China, China Hybrid, Noisette, Bourbon, Tea, Hybrid Perpetual, and 'Rivers's Musk' (rosy-buff, raised at Sawbridgeworth from Italian seed) is also included. Perhaps some had come from Michael Guilfoyle's Exotic Nursery at Double Bay in Sydney, who six years earlier had listed eighty 'really choice' imports, among them four from England: 'Captain Parry', 'Jupiter', 'La Tyre' and 'Miss Elliott'. Here 'Hebe's Lip' (a Bourbon hybrid) was considered one

ABOVE RIGHT
The Rosery, Botanical Gardens, Adelaide. Engraving from photograph by Captain Sweet, *The Australian Observer,* **1876**
(*supplied by Trevor Nottle*)

RIGHT
Climber 'Gloire de Dijon', from France in 1853, was deemed 'unquestionably the finest Tea Rose in cultivation' by John Rule's Nursery in Melbourne seven years later.

of the most beautiful roses ever grown and 'Maiden's Blush' a capital rose for a standard. Later, Guilfoyle's son, William, became curator of the Royal Botanic Gardens, Melbourne.

I have a list of roses grown there in 1889 and of the total of 273, two-thirds are Hybrid Perpetuals and the ten old summer flowerers included are made up of five Moss, three Damask and two Gallica. Today there is a much more representative selection in the Gardens and I found them extremely well presented in ten informal beds following historical sequence. The concise brochure is one of the best I have seen and for anybody wanting quickly to gain an outline of rose development, there is a full description, a simple rose family tree, as well as helpful diagrams of the present layout. I was there past the main flowering time but found some Teas and Rugosas blooming; with a particularly impressive display of hips in the four beds of species roses.

At the Botanic Garden of Adelaide I had the opportunity to study early records and learned that *R. eglanteria* (Sweet Briar) was introduced as an ornamental before 1839 and by the end of 1841 five specimens were growing in the old Botanic Gardens (*Journal of the Adelaide Botanic Garden* 6, 2, 1983). In 1859 twenty-three species were listed, with *R. rugosa* from Japan and *R. nitida* from North America evident by 1878. Accounts of 1866 showed that fifty rose stocks, twenty-four standard rose plants and 200 briars at 4s per hundred had been purchased from different sources: W. Lucas, Edwin Smith and D. Johns. As always, when searching through such papers, diversion is hard to resist (especially when invoiced in such perfect copperplate) and I noted six bushels of heath soil from James Carter of High Holborn, best peat soil from William Bull of Kings Road, Chelsea and a wide selection of garden periodicals from Dulan & Co., booksellers of Soho Square. Flower seeds were obtained from James Carter, a specialist in Essex, who also sent sphagnum moss. In 1872 the garden obtained from Stottbecker Baumschulen of Hamburg a selection of roses: 'Boursault Gracilis', 'Beauty of the Prairies', 'Noisette purpurea' and 'Dundee Rambler'. Two years later a Rugosa hybrid 'Regeliana' came from J. Linden in Belgium, the same being supplied by William Bull for 5s.

The first detailed invoice for roses at the Botanic Garden, dated 19 August 1881, was for six varieties from George Brunning of Melbourne's St Kilda Nurseries. It is not clear how many of each arrived, but having subsequently seen the illustration (p. 71) of the Garden's extensive Rosery from *The Australian Observer* (1876), it could have been a substantial order. I feel that those from Hamburg would most likely have been used for embellishment on the perimeter, as all are climbers, and certainly Brunning's would have been planted in the central beds. Being unfamiliar with his select half-dozen, I turned to my invaluable Shirley Hibberd, whose *The Amateur's Rose Book* (1894) has a comprehensive descriptive list of all known roses of the time. I found these all to be Hybrid Perpetuals of recent introduction.

Following is the Brunning list with price and, alongside, the Hibberd source (a good international representation) with, date and colour. With the exception of 'Mad. Jeanne Bouger', all are described as large and vigorous.

Penelope Mayo	7s 6d	Davis	(1878)	carmine
Mad. Jeanne Bouger	3s 6d	Gonod	(1877)	pink
Mad. Gabriel Luizit	3s 6d	Liabaud	(1877)	pink
Countess of Roseberry	7s 6d	Postans	(1879)	carmine
Richard Laxton	3s 6d	Laxton	(1878)	crimson
John Bright	5s 0d	Paul & Son	(1878)	scarlet

My next move was to pursue the connection between Thomas Rivers of Sawbridgeworth and Thomas Lang of Ballarat. This, as already mentioned, had been a great spur towards urging me to Australia and I arrived at Barney Hutton's home in Mount Macedon with eager anticipation. This is up in the hills behind Melbourne and I was there before the fires of 1983 when his garden and plantation of trees were completely destroyed. Now, he tells me, he has a jungle of seedling eucalypts 15 ft (4·5 m) high and Rugosas are blooming again. He had been researching early nurseries in the mining areas and I had a most rewarding time discussing nineteenth-century gardening in Victoria. Practically all that follows is compiled from lists he had laboriously copied by hand or photocopies of catalogues he had obtained for me, for which I am very grateful, and also to the Victoria State Library where they are held.

Thomas Lang emigrated from a nursery business in Kilmarnock, Scotland to establish one at Ballarat in Victoria, where sudden development following the discovery of gold led to urgent demand for fruit, vegetables and flowers, not only from local Australians, but also from a Chinese labour force. To meet the specialized demand he wrote to Hong Kong for appropriate vegetable seeds. He also imported rhododendron from the Far East, produced saleable hybrids and was the first to introduce *Lilium auratum* from Japan. Roses for the Lang nursery were obtained from fourteen sources between 1857 and 1867, some local and others overseas. One of his first suppliers was T. Adcock in Geelong, not to far away, and a record shows that with a dozen each of red and white Moss, 100 Sweet Briar, four 'White Cabbage', six 'Persian Yellow' and only four of one Hybrid Perpetual, 'Robin Hood', the older varieties were still very much in demand.

Other Australian nurseries to supply Lang with roses were Shepherd of Sydney and a number in the Melbourne area. Benjamin and Stephen Johnson, originally seed merchants from Preston, set up a business in Melbourne. By 1861 they were advertising numerous ornamental trees, shrubs, plants and roses, of which they sent to Lang a dozen each of 'Souvenir de la Malmaison' and 'Caroline de Sansal', an unnamed blush white Hybrid Perpetual, nine 'Devoniensis' and two of Paul's 'Queen Victoria', in a total of over 100 covering eighteen varieties. Their catalogue drew attention to 10,000 roses, mostly on their own roots, with 'Queen of the Prairies' and 'Harisonii' from the USA and 'Guilfoyle's XXX', a rich purple-crimson Hybrid Perpetual, presumably home-produced, among them. George Brunning, arriving in 1854 from Lowestoft in Suffolk, first managed John Rule's nursery in Melbourne and had established his own at St Kilda by 1860. Thirteen years later he was boasting of 'my very extensive collection of roses, which I believe is not

OVERLEAF LEFT
Amongst roses for exhibition, Thomas Johnson included one Gallica, 'Boule de Nanteuil' in *Culture of the Rose*, first account of rose growing in Victoria, 1866.

OVERLEAF RIGHT
Thomas Rivers classed 'Madame Hardy' as 'quite first amongst white roses'. This Damask long maintained a place in overseas nurseries as well.

approached, either in quantity or quality by any other nursery in the Southern Hemisphere'. The Lang records show that about eighty roses were received from him, all named and Hybrid Perpetuals predominating from 1866 to 1867.

English roses came from Rivers, E. P. Francis of Hertford, H. Lowe of Clapton and James Veitch of Exeter from 1858 to 1866. A Sawbridgeworth consignment, dispatched from England on 1 January 1858, arrived on 31 March and consisted of fifteen named varieties, totalling thirty-seven in all. Twenty-eight were Hybrid Perpetuals and two were the *R. sempervirens* Ramblers, 'Félicité Perpétue' and 'Adélaide d'Orléans', favourites of Rivers. An enormous number of fruit trees were also sent from his nursery: in 1861 on the SS *Great Britain* were 4,000 each of pear, cherry and crab, with 1,000 thorn, turkey oak and horse chestnut. Roses were also included in this prodigious consignment, but there was not a single Hybrid Perpetual among 100 Common Moss, fifty Old Cabbage, fifty White Provence, twelve Scotch and some Ayrshires. Perhaps this might indicate that newcomers were now more readily available in Australia than the older varieties.

A collection from E. P. Francis took longer to reach Ballerat from Hertford being dispatched before Christmas 1861 and not arriving until May 1862. Twenty varieties are named, though no quantity of each given, and among the predominating Hybrid Perpetuals were a Bourbon 'Catherine Guillot', Tea 'Louise de Savoie', and Noisette 'Triomphe de Rennes'. A rather laconic note refers to: 'William Paul, 8 December 1862 per mail steamer arr. 11 March 1863. Roses 63. 9 alive 23 May 1863', but no names of the stalwart survivors are given. Lowe's long list of sixty-seven named varieties, totalling about 150, were conveyed per SS *Royal Mail*, 11 June 1867, and forty unnamed roses arrived from James Veitch.

Thomas Lang's own catalogue (no. 39 for 1872) lists his roses under classes: Select Hybrid Perpetual (142), Bourbon (thirteen), Tea-Scented (nineteen), Noisette (five) and Miscellaneous (fifteen). In the last were four Moss and two Climbing Ayrshires, 'Eclipse' and 'Ruga', while the only Gallica was the striped 'Perle des Panachées'. Thirty-one standards were offered from 3s 6d to 5s each and other prices ranged from 1s to 3s 6d, with the exception of a Hybrid Perpetual, 'Leopold Hapsburg' (1864) and 'Maréchal Niel', from 2s to 3s. 'Gloire de Dijon' at 1s 6d showed that this had now become commonplace since John Rule had asked 5s for it in 1860, and glowingly described it as 'unquestionably the finest Tea Rose in cultivation'.

George Smith was another nurseryman at Ballarat. Before coming to Australia, he was employed in the Queen's Royal Fruit and Flower Gardens at Windsor Castle. His rose lists of 1861 and 1862 present 'Autumn Roses' and 'Summer Roses', very much in the Rivers tradition, and also offered a fine collection of pot roses, as would undoubtedly have been grown by him to embellish the Royal Household. In 1863 he published in Ballarat *The cottage gardener ... comprising the kitchen, fruit and flower garden*, an apt treatise for that community. Both Thomas Lang and George Smith were quoted in a recent comprehensive study, *Trees and Gardens from the Goldmining Era. A Study of the Maldon Landscape*, prepared by the Royal Botanic Gardens, Melbourne.

One of the first detailed accounts of rose growing in Victoria is given in *Culture of the Rose* (1866), and the author, Thomas Johnson, takes pains to emphasize the use of old roses for decorative garden display and exhibition, retaining more in his lists than Rivers. The American–French 'Madame Trudeaux' (see p. 29) appears among new Hybrid Perpetuals for 1866, described as deep rosy red; a comment of 'compact and beautiful' had come from the Handasyde McMillan Nursery in Melbourne two years earlier. To round off this brief resumé of some early Australian catalogues, Brunning's of 1898 claimed to have the largest collection in the southern hemisphere and listed some 250 Hybrid Perpetual, just overtaken by 260 Tea-Scented and Hybrids, plus fourteen Bourbon, twenty-four Noisette, twenty-two Moss, fifteen Hybrid Sweet Briar and fifty-seven miscellaneous. A report from New South Wales, published in *The Rose Annual*, 1908, judged 'Frau Karl Druschki', a pure white Hybrid Tea from Germany, 1901, the favourite of all foreign roses yet received.

R. roxburgii roxburgii is often seen in the Antipodes, its rather loose petals, deep pink in the centre, surrounded by paler.

Hybrid Sweet Briars, newcomers of the 1890s, were bred in England by Lord Penzance from *R. eglanteria* and of the sixteen listed by Graham Thomas in *Shrub Roses of Today* (1962), only two are missing from the Brunning catalogue. I was pleased to find the Damask 'York and Lancaster' in the miscellaneous list, also interested to see *R. pomifera* (now *R. villosa*) here suggested as attractive ornament for the garden, and others as camouflage for unsightly buildings or to create 'a grand effect mixed amongst other plants in the shrubbery or flower garden'; indications of a new gardening trend.

Diana Morgan of Heritage Roses took me to Mount Macedon and on the way pointed out 'Glenara' in Bulla as the family home of Alister Clark. Between 1914 and 1962 he bred 122 roses (*Heritage Roses in Australia*, vol 1, No. 3, 1979) and Tom Garnett, currently working on a Clark biography has supplied more details. When at Cambridge, he established contact with European rosarians, including William Paul, who later supplied him with *R. gigantea*, important in producing climbers suited to the hot, dry climate. He generously bestowed his roses on garden societies throughout Australia and allowed them to be propagated and sold for profit. Many were lost, but are being traced by Susan Irvine and established in an Alister Clark Garden at Malmsbury. Another, dedicated to his memory in St Kilda, has recently been replanted for further recognition of this rosarian, the first from overseas to gain the Dean Hole Medal from the National Rose Society of England in 1936.

When I look back to my short stay in South Australia, I must record my appreciation of help from Deane Ross and Trevor Nottle. The first, with his wife, Maureen, took me from Adelaide Airport to meet Alex Ross (who has since died), Deane's father, a rosarian well known internationally. He told me his grandfather had settled in South Australia in 1849 and his father, George, established Ross Roses Nursery in 1904, teaching him to bud at the age of six. Before the First World War he was using 'Adelaide Briar' stock for standards, a rose, his grandfather claimed, that quickly adapted to the demanding climate, and first used as stock fences on farms. Deane adds that 'Adelaide Briar' is rather different from other forms of *R. canina*: the rampant invader is now declared a nuisance weed, to be removed where practical. His father did much work on Alister Clark roses in the 1920s and 1930s and recollected 'Lorraine Lee' as one of the most popular. He took me round his garden, filled with roses, and showed me a treasured *R. roxburgii*, propagated from one he reckoned to be 100 years old at the home of his wife's parents.

In 1981 Deane moved Ross Roses to Willunga, thirty miles south of Adelaide. The nursery covered seventeen acres of former farmland and the display garden, always open to the public, now has 1,000 different varieties: over 600 'old-world' roses, over 200 moderns and 200 in various stages of testing. 'Sophie's Perpetual', from Sangerhausen, was in the quarantine area and I could tell Deane that this rose had reached East Germany from Humphrey Brooke's garden in England – a splendid example of a rose dispersed around the world.

Deane's practical account *Shrub Roses in Australia* (1981) has recently been updated and *Rose Growing for Pleasure* (Melbourne, 1985) is a concise, comprehensive survey, reflecting his genuine appreciation, particularly of roses in landscape gardening.

After a day in the library of the Botanic Garden of Adelaide, with kind advice from the Director, Brian Morley and others, Trevor Nottle took me to his home, Walnut Hill, in Stirling on the outskirts of Adelaide. I had heard of my second host's energy and enthusiasm, which were well demonstrated over the next couple of days as he took me to gardens of early mansions in the Mount Lofty area, across arid Mallee country to Renmark and through more lush corn and vine growing areas to Watervale. Trevor is an active member of the Garden History Society of Australia and has filled his garden with rare plants, integrating them with old and species roses. His book, *Growing Old-Fashioned Roses in Australia and New Zealand* (Kenthurst, 1983) is full of sound practical advice and aesthetic feeling. In 1979 he founded Heritage Roses in Australia by sending a circular to 100 people who had shown some interest in old roses; since then membership has risen to over 400. As in America, this society is run on unconventional lines, with co-ordinators for local groups based on cities and geographic zones and occasional organized activities, sometimes in conjunction with The National Trust of Australia, to conserve old rose sites in cemetery, churchyard, convict settlement or gold mining town. For some time Trevor edited the Society's stimulating journal, sending me many copies as well as other publications on garden history in Australia; all most helpful for this chapter.

David Ruston's seven-hectare nursery in the desert at Renmark, 160 miles north-east of Adelaide, is astonishing. Relying entirely on irrigation from the Murray River by inconspicuous underground plasting piping, he has become one of the principal suppliers of cut roses in Australia. The vast expanse of brilliant colour is broken by pillars of roses and vines, backed by well-placed trees; his father planted Lombardy poplar, golden elm and willow in 1922 and he has added more, some exotic, for necessary shelter. In the very dry heat there is no black spot to affect the roses and some produce six flushes of bloom a year. When I was there red and yellow were the most popular colours, but now I hear demand is for pastel pinks, creams and soft apricots. In a wilder area, many old roses are grown informally, the greyish foliage of *R. soulieana* providing a soft background for some, and a vast *R. × fortuniana* covers a large shed. David uses many of these smaller bloom roses for decorative indoor display, in which he excels.

The last nursery I visited in South Australia is in the grounds of Hughes Park, Watervale, a mansion built between 1867 and 1873 and now home of Walter Duncan and his family. There, along a fronting balustrade, 'Cloth of

Gold', with a massive bole, has trailed its way for a century and I was also intrigued to see the original flower and fruit gardens enclosed with 'walls' of solid old olive trees. There is a good selection of Victorian roses in the display garden. Walter uses 'Dr Huey' as understock and all the newly budded roses have vertical netting hung between the rows as a deterrant to destructive parrots and for protection from wind damage to new shoots. He finds speedy budders from abroad an economic investment and told me that other growers employ them from Mexico, South America and Europe.

When staying with friends in Victoria I collected some miscellaneous comments for my rose notebook. At Delatite, home of the Ritchies, near Mansfield, 'Fortune's Yellow', a massive, gnarled centenarian, covers one side of the house and a classical formal rose garden is outlined by neat little box hedges. Broad borders curve round the lawns, while 'La France' and 'Souvenir de Madame Léonie Viennot', favoured old roses, happily associate with carefully selected herbaceous plants, 'Sea Foam' surges among shrubs and 'Wedding Day' cascades from an old tree in this spacious, lovely garden sloping to the river. In another nearby, I was shown 'Aunt Bette's Rose' and 'The Ennerdale Rose' of local naming, probably a Hybrid Perpetual and a China, but thus they will always be known. An imposing garden near Melbourne with an admirable collection of old roses, is approached through a wonderful white avenue of *Eucalyptus citriodora* and there I was interested to see the site of a rose garden by Edna Walling, the Australian designer (1896–1973), on the lines of Gertrude Jekyll planning. Joan Law-Smith writes about her beautiful Macedon garden, Bolobek, with great sensitivity and so it is planted, with roses of quiet colour, 'Boule de Neige' prominent in a white arrangement. At Rippon Lea, one of Melbourne's great Victorian mansions now administered by The National Trust, I learned of plans to replant the original roses which visitors would have seen when alighting at the ornate *porte-cochère* or walking through the extensive gardens to the cool, slatted fernery. All these gardens, in their diversity, play a part in contributing to Australia's rose history.

Since I was in South Australia, the Second International Heritage Rose Conference has been held in Adelaide (1986) and one outcome is a proposal to establish a repository of tender old roses at the Waite Agricultural Research Institute in the city. This followed a suggestion by Peter Beales, principal guest speaker, who has offered to co-ordinate collections of Teas, Chinas and old cold-sensitive varieties from sources in Europe and England and to send them to Australia for safe-keeping. Periodically there will be an opportunity to view these roses and budwood will be made available to international collectors. This remarkable project had emanated from Trevor Nottle's letter written within the last decade and must augur well for other exciting developments through Heritage Rose Societies to conserve and redistribute varieties otherwise lost to posterity.

First of Hybrid Tea Roses, 'La France' (1867), with high centre and soft pink reflexed petals, still flowers in many Australian gardens today.

CHAPTER 9

Roses Flourish in New Zealand

PERHAPS one reason why China Roses were to be found in the earliest gardens of North Island, New Zealand was because they were marketed in pots and thus readily available for long distance transport at any time of the year. It is known that the 'Crimson China' was growing in gardens in the far north some time before 1822, when cuttings of it were taken from the early landing place at Oihi to Keri Keri for the garden of historic Kemp House, the oldest wooden dwelling preserved in New Zealand. This was to be occupied by George Clarke, father of another George destined to become Archdeacon of Tasmania. Seventy years on he recalled the time when together they went into the garden, picked a half-open bud of a Cabbage Rose and placed it in the hand of a baby girl, dead through whooping cough. This incident always returned 'with the sight and smell of cabbage roses and is a sort of faint musk to my memory'. (*Notes on Early Life in New Zealand*, Hobart, 1903).

China and old summer roses thrived in the temperate climate and in November 1835 a recently arrived missionary wife commented on the dwelling of another at Pahia: 'A pretty cottage, a verandah in front through which woodbines and roses most luxuriantly twine. What we consider beautiful roses in England grow here almost as weeds.' The following month Charles Darwin also called in and remarked, 'At Pahia it was quite pleasing to behold the English flowers in the platforms before the houses; there were roses of several kinds, honeysuckle, jasmine, stocks and whole hedges of sweet briar.' At the mission station further south, Te Papa in the Bay of Plenty, the Rev. A. N. Brown, later Archdeacon of Tauranga, first lived in a small raupo (rush) cottage protected by hedges and sheltered belts, described by visiting Bishop Selwyn as 'a pretty cottage of native workmanship, surrounded by rose trees, all looking comfortable and suitable'. In 1848 the family moved into The Elms, a staunch mission house, built with wood from the northern kauri forests, and still in immaculate condition today. It seems that a garden had been prepared in advance as Celia, the Brown daughter wrote that year, 'the first cabbage roses were picked on 7 November and the first damask rose came out two days later'.

Judge Chapman and his wife, Catherine, came to New Zealand in 1844 and settled in Karori, now a suburb of Wellington. He wrote of the garden: 'Kate's outdoor nursery is as flourishing as *her* nursery. We prize it for the many English plants that are doing well. You would laugh to see how we watch and cherish a bramble, an elder bush, two furze bushes, a dozen oaks and a dozen sweetbriars.' However, it was not long before gardens were looking like those left far away. 'It is, I suppose, rather characteristic of an English Colony that the gardens here are full of English plants and roses,' wrote Charlotte, wife of John Godley, Chief Agent of the Canterbury Association, from Wellington in 1850 and she described the garden of the house they were renting before proceeding south. It was, she said, 'Really very pretty, only a little out of order; with sweet briar, honeysuckle, clove pinks and white moss roses and the other real English plants, scarcely yet out of flower and overrun with fuchsias, which make hedges, almost.'

From her letters more is learned of roses in the early 1850s. She found necessary shelter lacking in Canterbury and towards the end of the year wrote, 'Those settlers who came out in ships touching at the Cape generally brought supplies of flowers and shrubs from there and they all do uncommonly well – and even bear the wind pretty well – which the roses do not!' In November 1851 they were visiting the home of the Resident Magistrate at Akaroa on the Banks Peninsula, passing through 'a very neat gate up a nicely kept little patch of lawn, a beautiful stream on one side and on the other a high hedge of roses, the monthly ones in full blow, and the cabbage, provence, etc. just beginning'. On returning to her home in Lyttleton, she seemed pleased and found it 'quite cheering to see the garden looking quite green, giving good promise of everything; the little bits of sweet briar that were sent me some months ago from Wellington were positively sweet, and full of leaf and so were the rose-trees. We do not aspire to flowers for this year'.

Lady Butler's *Station Life in New Zealand* (1870, reprinted London, 1984) was published in the form of letters to her sister in England. Although married for a second time, to a Mr Broome, she kept her previous name and they lived at Broomielaw, a remote sheep station in the Malvern Hills, north of Christchurch. She writes of visiting distant neighbours, where she was up and out on the verandah as early as possible saying constantly in a sort of ecstasy,

> How I wish they could see this in England and not only see but *feel* it, for the very breath one draws on such a morning is happiness; the air is so light and yet balmy it seems to heal the lungs as you inhale it. The verandah is covered with honeysuckles and other creepers and the gable end of the house, where the bow window of the drawing room projects, is one mass of yellow Banksia roses in full blossom.

That was in November 1865 and I recollect, some ninety years on, feeling exactly the same on my first morning at Ohakea; relishing the clarity of distant views, almost sparkling air and pure notes of bird song. In November of the following year, 'an easy 12 mile ride on horseback' took Lady Butler to a charming little station where established willows, gum trees and poplars provided shelter for the 'large wide verandah round two sides of the house with French windows opening on to it and I could not help feeling impatient to see my own creepers in such luxuriant beauty as those roses and honeysuckles were'.

These are just three of the many pioneering ladies who led the way in their new country's enthusiasm for gardening. Later in the century, Mrs. Adela Stewart of Athenree, Bay of Plenty – a far more benign region than the Canterbury Plains – described her gardening activities from 1878 to 1906 in *My Simple Life in New Zealand* (Auckland 1908). Here roses could be grown more ambitiously: 'A blue gum and a Cloth of Gold rose cutting, side by side, had a close race, so that when we left 24 years later, they had attained a height of the gum 100 ft [30·3 m] and the rose 60 ft [18 m]. They were in beautiful

One of Auckland's historic houses open to the public, Ewelme Cottage, 1886, has a yellow Banksian to the left of the steps.
(*Courtesy of Auckland Institute and Museum*)

entanglement – the admiration of the countryside.' This Noisette seems to have been a universal favourite in the nineteenth century, making spectacular displays the world over.

Perhaps in the decorative aspect of growing roses, these New Zealand ladies may have been ahead of those in the country they had left. Because of searing winds in Canterbury and before tree-belt shelter had become established, houses provided the only protection so that verandahs were festooned with roses and other climbing plants. Looking at Mrs Stewart's picture of the flower garden at Athenree in North Island, seeing it merging into woodland – just the sort of scene beloved by Gertrude Jekyll, I am certain Mrs Stewart would not have planted her roses in beds (and none are mentioned in her show exhibits) but would have arranged them, as with the 'Cloth of Gold', beautifully among her trees and shrubs, as was the vogue of the Edwardians.

John Edgerley, a knowledgeable botanist and gardener in New Zealand from 1835, was instrumental in arranging an exchange of plants with England and in 1842 took over a consignment for Sir William Hooker at Kew. In a letter to the Royal Gardens before his return, he requests many flowering shrubs, 'with a few good roses, white moss if you can spare it'. It would seem that these were for the nursery he then set up in Newmarket, Auckland. At the first show of the Auckland Agricultural and Horticultural Society, December 1843, a Mr Clarke gained an award for strawberries, a Moss Rose and a hollyhock. By the 1857 show, Victorian roses had become established and the Governor's gardener, Mr Lynch, exhibited a prizewinning 'Madame Laffay', one of the first Hybrid Perpetuals to be raised in France in 1839.

Nancy Steen, writing on 'Old Roses in New Zealand a Hundred Years Ago' (in *The New Zealand Rose Annual*, 1965), takes as her guide a list of fifty-seven roses from Hale of Nelson dated 1860, twelve of which were sent north to Auckland. By this time roses from England were arriving regularly in Australia and it is probable that some of them came to Nelson on the direct route from Hobart or Sydney to Wellington. In 1865 Hale's list had increased to seventy-six and it is interesting to note that among the many Hybrid Perpetuals, two more Gallicas had arrived; 'Perle des Panachées ('Cottage Maid') (1845) and 'Tricolore de Flandre' (1846), both variegated, to make an attractive quartet with 'Tricolore' (1840) and 'Gloire de France' (1828) on the earlier list.

At the 1859 Auckland Show, David Hay of Montpellier Nursery gained many prizes for vegetables, shrubs and trees. His 1863 catalogue (thought by S. Challenger to be the first extant in New Zealand when I was last in touch with him) listed twenty-four roses in five classes: Hybrid Perpetual, Île de Bourbon, Noisette, Tea-Scented and China and also mentioned another, Hybrid China, as an extensive group of almost any colour, to be grown in any soil and to be pruned sparingly. 'Running Roses' for covering walls and 'Banksian Roses' were not named, but 'Monettia' (Manetti) was advocated as a fine stock for budding or grafting Tea-Scented Roses. There is no note of price in this catalogue, but two years later a selection of thirty-six roses ranged from 5s for the most expensive, 'Miss Alice Gray', a true Noisette, to the 'Crimson China' and 'Scotch Rose' for 1s. In 1867 Hybrid Perpetuals were divided into two sections (I cannot see why as the same colours and prices, from 2s and 1s 6d appear in both), the price of 'Miss Alice Gray' has been halved, while 'Cloth of Gold' has only dropped 6d to 3s 6d. Five years on, the Hay catalogue

'Tricolore de Flandre', a
variegated Gallica of
1846, included in a list
from William Hale of
Nelson in 1865.

R. banksiae Lutea,
frequently mentioned in
letters, enjoyed the
shelter of verandahs of
early New Zealand
Homes.

lists one rose under the Provence heading: 'Cabbage' at 1s to 2s and now, under Noisettes, 'Maréchal Niel' is deemed a decided improvement on 'Cloth of Gold' while 'Miss Alice Gray' has disappeared. By the turn of the century the Hay catalogue had become very comprehensive, covering some 250 roses and even four new Hybrid Teas, cost no more than 2s 6d each.

Copies of Hay catalogues were sent to me by S. Challenger, whose work on early Canterbury nurserymen had appeared in *Garden History* (Vol. III, No. 1, London, 1974 and Vol. VII, No. 1, 1979). From that and a further piece in the *Annual Journal of the Royal New Zealand Institute of Horticulture*, (No. 7, 1979), I have gleaned information on early roses in the Christchurch nurseries. William Wilson led the field and with the vital importance of protection from wind sweeping over the vast Canterbury Plains, he was offering in 1851, 'Sweet Bryar thorn, privet and gorse for hedging'. A substantial advertisement in the *Southern Provinces Almanac* (1863) offered forest trees, hedging plants, fruit trees, flowering plants in pots, herbaceous plants and 'blooming roses in fifteen select varieties'. John Greenaway in the Papanui Road concentrated on them, winning many prizes at shows of the Christchurch Horticultural Society and contributing prize money for extended classes during the 1860s, as well as advertising 'The Finest Varieties in Cultivation' in the 1869 *Almanac*. This enthusiasm led to his untimely death in 1882 from a fall when endeavouring to pass from one moving tramcar to another, with 'an unusually fine rose in his hand' to show to the treasurer of the Horticultural Society. Mrs Greenaway carried on his work, renaming the business, now in Victoria Street, 'The Rosary' and specializing in roses, flower and vegetable seeds, for which she issued a free catalogue.

Andrew Duncan, a horticulturist and nursery gardener from Scotland, first set up as a seed merchant in Gloucester Street before moving to establish 'exotic nurseries' in Ferry Road and issuing his first catalogue in 1879 containing 'a wide range of roses'. This called special attention of rose-growers to recently imported varieties: fifteen Hybrid Perpetuals, two Tea-Scented at 5s ('Bouton d'Or' and 'Madame Margottin') as well as a large stock of the splendid 'Maréchal Niel' at 3s 6d. Thomas Abbott from Devon founded his Exeter Nurseries in Papanui Road and advertised in the *Christchurch Horticultural Society Show Schedule* (1881): 'Thousands of Roses (very choice) to which I have added by Importation, upwards of a Hundred Varieties'. These references will show that within thirty years roses in great selection were available in the Christchurch area.

In the far south, nurserymen of Dunedin, George Matthews, Robert Thomson and Thomas Allen were offering a wide choice of roses in their catalogues by the 1870s. Matthews headed his 1876 collection with planting instructions; advocating well manuring the ground to a depth of 2 ft (60 cm) and then placing a layer of 6–7 in (15–17·5 cm) of sand over the roots to keep the soil uniformly moist, prevent weeds and promote better flowering. He considered 'Madame William Paul' the best perpetual Moss yet introduced and included it among his five specialities: three Teas and a climbing variety of 'Victor Verdier', winner of a first-class certificate from the Horticultural Society of London. Among Thompson's 170 roses offered in 1876 the most expensive, at 5s, were five new Teas, three Hybrid Perpetuals and a Noisette 'Bouquet d'Or' and while Allen praised the Tea, 'Bouton d'Or', he reckoned

'Maréchal Niel' still to be the finest yellow rose for the 1878–9 season.

Later catalogues indicate how prices fell by the end of the nineteenth century. In 1882 Nairn and Sons of Christchurch issued a Special Price List in which their collection of 150 roses 'containing most of the leading varieties suitable for exhibition or general decoration purposes' cost 10s to 15s per dozen. The same publication ten years later priced 174 Hybrid Perpetuals at 9s per dozen or 1s each; Teas, Hybrid Teas and Noisettes were 12s per dozen, with the exception of seven new ones at 2s 6d or 2s each and miscellaneous Hybrid China, Banksian and Moss at 1s. Finally, Horton's Premier Nurseries of Pahiatua issued an 1899 list containing 'most of the sterling novelties of recent introduction . . . imported more for their real worth than their newness here'. There were still almost as many Hybrid Perpetuals (around seventy) as all the other classes put together, maintaining their price, although Tea-Scented and their Hybrids had dropped to 10s per dozen. Seven Polyanthas now warranted a separate list at 1s to 1s 6d each and, among the miscellaneous, 'Madame George Bruant', one of the new Rugosa hybrids, with the Tea 'Sombreuil' as a parent, was described as a valuable pure white decorative rose. Horton still offered six Mosses and at the end of his selective list he stressed that any roses not catalogued could be supplied, thus underlining the high standard of rose growing in New Zealand by the end of the century – and one that continued, as I appreciated when I returned there in 1982.

I had lived as a Royal Air Force wife first at Ohakea and then in Khandallah, Wellington, from 1952 to 1955, three very happy years, although at that time I had no involvement with old roses (rather with sweet peas, my husband's speciality, and we made many a trip to Lower Hutt to collect seaweed for their trenches). My second visit, coinciding almost thirty years to the day from when we came by sea to Wellington, was entirely taken up with them, from the moment that I was able to detect my hostess by a bouquet of Bourbon 'Souvenir de la Malmaison' waving high above the waiting crowd at Auckland Airport, to the day I flew off into the evening sun from Christchurch with a nosegay of Noisettes to remind me of Akaroa. The greeting had been cut from the Sylvesters' garden at Greenhithe, acquired in 1971 and named 'Omahanui' (place of pleasure) in anticipation of their skill with an untended wilderness. Now, Teas grow to immense proportions: 'Jean Ducher', 'Souvenir de Madame Léonie Viennot' and 'Devoniensis' among them, and smaller roses are associated charmingly in mixed borders, where I found a surprising sport of 'Dorcas', with variegated foliage, called 'Achievement'.

Toni Sylvester has since told me of further ambitious improvements to one of the few private gardens open to the public in New Zealand. She took me to see Nancy Steen, leading expert on old roses in the southern hemisphere, who told me of her commitment to worldwide correspondence now that she no longer could work in the garden. Her husband showed me 'Lamarque', high in silver birches, a white collection secreted on a lower level and, significant with her old treasures, 'Nancy Steen', bred in New Zealand in the 1970s, from 'Ophelia', a rose aptly named, with abundant creamy-pink blooms. After speaking to Heritage Roses members I was taken by the President, Ken Nobbs to his 'Rosery' at Te Kauwhata, some 60 km south of Auckland, where since 1973 he has converted derelict agricultural land into a garden of billowing roses and fruitful trees. He also has many side pursuits: researching into

scented foliage, thornlessness, Vitamin C in hips, proposals to create a museum of historical plants and to plant rambler roses along main highways, as well as writing profusely.

I spent Christmas with Rhoda McWhannell, then in her eighties, whose enquiring mind and wonderful memory have contributed much to my story. She told me of Joy Fillery, a late friend, and her beautiful garden in a valley west of the Waipa, north of Hamilton, described in a booklet, *Old Fashioned Roses in New Zealand* (Ilfracombe, 1960), given to me by her daughter, who had gathered together enthusiastic gardeners of the Waikato District for an evening meeting. Rhoda and I visited public rose gardens; found many old varieties in Hamilton's and brilliant moderns at Te Awamutu, surrounding a lovely fountain of shimmering birds rising through a mist, created by Fred Graham, a Maori sculptor. We searched for roses by the roadside (an aspect well covered by Nancy Steen) and found 'Lady Gay' in abundance, 'The Bishop' past flowering in Paterangi Road and I learned of 'The Ohaupo Rose', discovered by a railway line.

I also saw roses running wild in Canterbury; 'Mermaid', 'Félicité Perpétue' and many Ramblers far away from present habitation. Here I was looked after by Kaye Stokes, another staunch member of Heritage Roses, taken to Hagley Park Botanic Garden, Mona Vale and private gardens in Christchurch, finding roses flowering much later than in the north, and driven over the Banks Peninsula Hills to Akaroa. The French came here in 1840 to found a settlement to provision their whaling fleet, then active in the South Pacific, but the British had already established sovereignty and further development was shared, as is evident from French names. Roses abound, particularly Chinas, neatly planted by picket fences. Jessie Mould, a great authority on local history and old roses, told me that Banksian Roses, yellow and white, pour from the Lombardy poplars in spring. She has named her cottage after them and a profusion of roses in the garden includes pale, almost single Bourbon, 'Souvenir de St Anne's', sport of 'Souvenir de la Malmaison', discovered in Ireland. We also called in at the Duvauchelle Cemetery, where many interesting roses, including Noisettes, have been found.

One of the highlights of my New Zealand trip was a visit to Trevor Griffiths at Temuka, South Canterbury, where a great collection of old and species roses flourish in what appeared to me to be a very dry display garden. However, in spite of low rainfall in summer, Trevor does not irrigate. He believes that about 300 varieties of the rose were brought over to New Zealand in early days, a static number until the 1960s, since when imports have increased the total to 1500, of which he grows 90 per cent in his nursery, many from Australia, Denmark, West Germany, the UK and the USA. His book, *My World of Old Roses* (Christchurch, 1983) was one of the first to illustrate so many varieties with concise descriptive notes and a second, *The Book of Classic Old Roses*, (London, 1986), was reviewed in *The Rose* of September 1987 by Michael Gibson, past President of the Royal National Rose Society, and its author commended for revealing so many hitherto unknowns. This entirely endorses my own impression of New Zealand's dedication and I believe the country must prove an exciting repository of old roses.

On the way back from Temuka, Kaye took me to see 'Charlie' (as he likes to be called) Challenger, now retired to Okuti Valley and more occupied with his

ABOVE LEFT
'Sombreuil', a Tea of 1850 with the look of an old rose, thrives in hot summers of the Antipodes and the United States.

LEFT
Amongst many beautiful Teas in the Auckland garden of Toni Sylvester, a founder of Heritage Roses New Zealand, 'Souvenir de Madame Léonie Viennot' grows vigorously.

In South Canterbury Display Garden of Trevor Griffiths, Gallica, 'Anaïs Ségales', fades from deep crimson to lilac.

own catalogue as an alpine nurseryman than with those of the past. I spent an interesting morning with Barry Eagle, then President of the New Zealand Rose Society, and his wife, Dawn, specialists in miniature roses at Southern Cross Nurseries, Christchurch. Thousands of tiny cuttings in a mist-propagation-house root in three weeks, to be widely dispatched by mail in pots and I was very pleased to hear of enthusiasm for introducing old-rose qualities of colour, scent and mossiness, and of their exchange with Ralph Moore, America's great authority on miniature roses.

I knew Nigel and Judy Pratt in the 1950s, but did not have a chance to visit their Tasman Bay Roses Nursery – established at Motueka, South Island in 1964 – although I feel I know their roses through an attractive and interesting catalogue, which includes a few not to be found in English lists at the moment. I wonder whether some could have originated from Upper Moutere, one of the first settlements in New Zealand of Lutheran missionaries from around Hamburg in the 1830s, who, being keen gardeners, may have brought roses from Europe, to be cherished by their descendants. Some still occupy the original houses and farms on this good agricultural land with plenty of rainfall, although the Pratts do find wind a hazard.

Frank Mason is a rose and fuchsia specialist at Feilding, North Island and Sam McGredy, the outstanding rose breeder, moved across the world from Ulster in 1972 to make New Zealand the birthplace of many important new roses for international distribution, thus reversing the North to South traffic of Victorian times.

Those early days are very much the concern of Heritage Roses, New Zealand, founded in 1980 by Toni Sylvester and Ken Nobbs, now with a membership of 800, a businesslike committee and an excellently produced quarterly journal. Their objective is to share information and enjoyment of old roses, members being responsible for city plantings, search in cemeteries and abandoned sites, as well as propagation and exchange of cuttings throughout the country. In the temperate climate, Teas and Chinas flourish in all but the coldest areas, some flowering throughout the year. A most successful weekend seminar on the identification of unknown Teas was held in Hawkes Bay in 1987. This enterprising Society organized the First International Conference on Old Roses at Hawera in December 1984 and the Fourth is to be held in Christchurch in 1990 with Kaye Stokes as Convenor.

Heritage Roses New Zealand recognizes the importance of Nancy Steen's book and has commemorated her name in the Nancy Steen Garden at the Rose Gardens, Gladstone Road, Parnell, Auckland, where a collection of old roses and companion plants are grown together in the way she loved. This was opened in November 1984 by Lady Beattie, wife of the Governor General, in Nancy Steen's presence. A year after her death in 1986, *The Charm of Old Roses* was reprinted; it is well worth reading, not only for a comprehensive account of them in New Zealand, but also for her gleanings from international travels and contacts.

Part IV

EDWARDIAN EMBELLISHMENT

The rambling and free-growing Roses seem to be offered to us by a specially benevolent horticultural providence.

GERTRUDE JEKYLL, *Roses for English Gardens* (1902)

'Dorothy Perkins'

CHAPTER 10

Roses Beautifully Used

THE first decade of the twentieth century brought a turnabout in rose fashion from the Victorian emphasis on large, spectacular blooms for competition in shows. Those roses of wondrous size, shade and fragrance often needed protection against inclement weather and consequently were sometimes covered up with protective cones, straw hats or umbrellas. The role of the rose as garden ornament was neglected, a point emphasized by Edwardian writers; their exhortations for a reconsideration of rose growing were substantiated by the availability of exciting new varieties, of which there had been spasmodic developments from France, the USA and England in the nineteenth century.

Potential qualities of a species rose of vigorous growth and graceful form led M. Jacques, one of the French royal gardeners, to collect seed from *R.*

sempervirens and other roses. This rose, from the Mediterranean area has an almost evergreen foliage, as its name indicates, and produces tenacious hybrids of invasive habit, two of which have since maintained a place in catalogues throughout the world: 'Adélaide d'Orléans (1826) is well displayed over an archway· at the National Trust's rose garden at Mottisfont, while 'Félicité Perpétue' must be one of the most widely used old rambling roses, tolerant even of a northern aspect.

In 1835 an amateur enthusiast in England, a Mr Wells of Tunbridge Wells, introduced two rambling roses using, it is thought, *R. moschata* × *R. multiflora* for 'The Garland' and reversing the parents for 'Madame d'Arblay'. The former was a great favourite of Gertrude Jekyll and is still popular, though 'Madame' makes but rare appearances – and the only one I have seen graces an old apple tree at Mottisfont. However, it was known early in the USA and called by Robert Buist 'Wells' White Climber', deemed very hardy and vigorous and thought by him a possible good stock rose. Samuel Feast's work with *R. setigera* in Baltimore, already mentioned, followed in the 1840s.

Both William Paul and Thomas Rivers were enthusiastic about Ayrshire Roses as, indeed, is Peter Beales today. There has been some debate over their origin, but the wild British climber, *R. arvensis*, is recognized as an ancestor. Paul stressed their suitability for converting 'the dreary waste into a flowery plain' and listed seven, including three white: 'Bennet's Seedling', 'Dundee Rambler' and 'Queen of the Belgians', a flesh-coloured 'Ruga', and 'Splendens' (also known as 'Myrrh-scented'), opening flesh from crimson buds, which he considered one of the best for a large weeping rose. Rivers used a 'Blush Ayrshire' with the dark Gallica 'Tuscany' to produce his 'Ayrshire Queen', claiming it to be the only dark one of its kind and recommending it as a good pillar rose. I discover from my overseas catalogues that Ayrshire Roses were available from four Canadian nurseries between 1853 and 1873, where they would have found an equitable climate – 'Queen of the Belgians' seems the variety most frequently offered. In Australia, however, I could only find 'Splendens' from Baptist of Sydney in 1861 with 'Ruga' from Lang of Ballarat in 1872 and hopes of some for sale in Dunedin in the far south of New Zealand with weather akin to Scotland's, proved unfounded.

R. multiflora was one of two species to play the most important part in producing rambling roses for the Edwardians. The first of this strain, from Japan, was introduced by Charles Turner of Slough, England, in 1893, to become known as 'Turner's Crimson Rambler'. Nothing like it had ever been seen before; impact was immediate, raising ecstatic comment from nurserymen the world over and, described as 'the floral wonder of the century', it appeared on the cover of Henderson's New York catalogue for 1895. Customers were assured they might invest in this hardy Japanese climbing rose with complete confidence – 'every garden in America should have at least one' – and, as an inducement, purchasers of their main collections would be presented with a strong young bush. The 1896 catalogue gave it another full page illustration and announced that after a year's trial, though essentially for the garden, it made a magnificent specimen in a pot or tub.

Brunning of Melbourne showed an illustration of what he called a 'new hardy Japanese polyantha rose' in 1898, saying it had been tested in their nursery during the last three summers, had been greatly admired and

RIGHT
Early Rambler, 'Madame d'Arblay', from Mr. Wells of Tunbridge Wells, Kent, 1835; here seen at Mottisfont.

succeeded best in cool districts. In his 1899–1900 catalogue Hay of Auckland also pictured 'Crimson Rambler', by then an 'old favourite' and offered to include it, for 4s the lot, with three new Ramblers to make up a colourful quartet. These were early Multiflora hybrids from Schmitt of Lyon, known as 'The Three Graces': the first, yellow, a cross with 'Rève d'Or' called 'Aglaia', pink 'Euphrosyne' and white 'Thalia'.

Also included in Hay's list of new roses and warranting his longest description was *R. wichuraiana*: 'Creeps on the ground like ivy, growing 20 feet [6 m] in one season, forming a dense mat of dark green lustrous foliage; invaluable for covering banks, extremely hardy, will grow in sun or shade; produces numberless satiny-white flowers, with yellow discs; adapts itself to all soils and conditions of growth. A rare novelty.' This paragon, at 1s 6d and the second prolific parent of Ramblers, had been discovered by a German botanist in Japan (and later named for him) some twenty years before plants were sent from Germany to the Arnold Arboretum in the USA in 1888. There it was propagated and distributed to nurserymen and to Kew. By 1896 it was on the back cover of Henderson, as 'The Memorial Rose', when 50,000 were purchased by park and cemetery superintendents in the New York area and it was being used 'throughout the famous park system of Boston for covering rocky slopes and embankments ... hardy as grass'. While this proved invaluable in public planting, its hybrids were even more enthusiastically sought for gardens.

Pitcher and Manda of South Orange, New Jersey, first introduced Multiflora creations from Michael Horvath's use of 'Cramoisi Superieur' the red China, and 'Paquerette', a white Polyantha. Their 1899 catalogue extolled the virtues of 'Manda's Triumph', 'Universal Favourite', 'South Orange Perfection' and 'Pink Roamer' (a Sweet Briar hybrid) as an already proven quartet and introduced an outstanding trio. 'Jersey Beauty' and 'Gardenia' were single and double Ramblers from a liaison of *R. wichuraiana* with the beautiful yellow Tea Rose, 'Perle des Jardins' and 'Evergreen Gem' came from 'Madame Hoste', a Tea of rosy complexion. However, probably the most

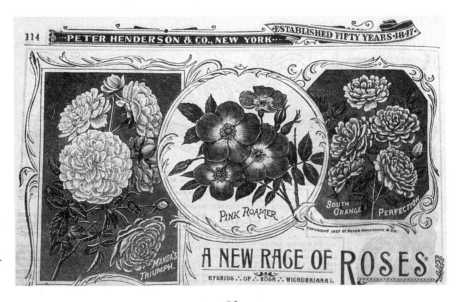

Praise for new Wichuraiana Ramblers in Henderson's *Manual of Everything for the Garden*, New York, 1897.
(Courtesy of Huntington Botanical Library)

famous of American Ramblers was brought out by Jackson & Perkins in 1910 and 'Dorothy Perkins' was soon providing pink cascades the world over. Other popular varieties from many Ramblers coming from the nursery of Walsh at Woods Hole were 'Lady Gay', 'Minnehaha' and 'Excelsa', also known as 'Red Dorothy Perkins'. Van Fleet's ubiquitous 'American Pillar', white-centred red, was followed by 'Dr W. van Fleet', whose sport 'New Dawn' (1930) must surely be one of the most successful of Wichuraiana roses. Very soon these Americans were crossing the Atlantic and those of European breeding made the journey in the opposite direction.

In France, Barbier of Orleans had been working on new roses of this strain and between 1901 and 1909, 'Alberic Barbier', 'Paul Transon', 'François Juranville' and 'Alexandre Girault' appeared, although 'Albertine', certainly the most popular Barbier rose in England, was not on the market until 1921. An interesting product of this nursery was 'Wichmoss' (1909) and when I came across it clinging to a low wall, there was no mistaking the little blush blooms, with mossy buds and glossy leaves, unfortunately prone to mildew.

Breeders in England were busy also: 'Blush Rambler' from Cant, with 'Crimson Rambler' and 'The Garland' as parents, was, and still is, one of the best. 'Paul's Scarlet' proved most popular at the time and his 'Goldfinch' was useful where less vigour was required. 'Sanders White' has always been valued for fragrance and 'Emily Gray', from Williams, of 'Jersey Beauty' extraction, proved a reliable yellow. Schmidt of Germany was responsible for 'Tausends-chön', of moderate height with pink–white blooms rather larger than most other Ramblers, a very good rose for pillars, and 'Veilchenblau', one of the first of the lovely lavender-purples emanating from 'Turner's Crimson Rambler'. Then 'Veilchenblau' in its turn produced 'Rose-Marie Viaud' of the 1920s, a contemporary of 'Violette', another Multiflora with good clusters of purplish blooms. The value of 'Turner's Crimson Rambler' lies in its progeny. Although it made great early impact, it has no scent and is prone to mildew.

In his *Art and Craft of Garden Making* (London, 1900), T. H. Mawson wrote on climbing roses and championed the older Scotch Climbers, 'Dundee Rambler' and 'Bennett's Seedling', notwithstanding recent improvements. However, he also acknowledged that 'Crimson Rambler' was invaluable for breaking up plantations of evergreen with pillars of brilliant colour. Although this was not one of her favourites, there can be no doubt that Gertrude Jekyll had new Edwardian Ramblers in mind when she remarked in the Preface to *Roses for English Gardens* (London, 1902) that the time had come 'when there is a distinct need for a book that shall not only show how Roses may best be grown, but how they may be beautifully used'. Photographs throughout illustrate this point and she emphasized it yet again at a Rose Conference held at Holland House the same year when she spoke specifically on the subject. Around this time, too, she contributed an article, 'The Garden Roses' to the *Journal of the Royal Horticultural Society*, stressing that rosarians of only twenty years before would have been very surprised to find so many classes of garden roses at the current shows. She added that the old roses could now be valued: Pink China, Provence, Moss, Damask and fine old rambling Ayrshires, side by side with new Ramblers and beautiful hybrids of various parentage. All these provided opportunities for use in beds and borders, as isolated specimens on pillars, pergolas, trellis, trees, rock gardens, walls, and banks and, finally,

'Apple Blossom', vigorous Multiflora Rambler,
quickly covered a post and rail fence in West Sussex
with large trusses of bloom.

LEFT   'Crimson Shower', late-flowering Rambler,
echoes original 'Crimson Rambler' in colour, but is
far healthier.

Gertrude Jekyll judged 'Blanc Double de Coubert' best of new Rugosa hybrids and liked its polished, persisting foliage.

'roses for the stately terraces of refined architecture and for such beautiful rose gardens as have never yet been made'. She stressed the importance of recent developments in rose growing in relation to a new desire to interpret their overall potential: now the close-up portrait was to be replaced by a landscape picture. I refer readers to her book, recently reprinted by the Antique Collectors Club (1982) and shall mention here only briefly some of her comments relevant to this section on the new rose concept.

The Jekyll colour-conscious eye is critical of the harsh red of 'Crimson Rambler' by day, although observes it mellows by evening sunlight. Both 'Dundee Rambler' and 'The Garland' are frequently mentioned, the latter pictured six times and viewed at 4 a.m. on a mid-June morning 'to see the tender loveliness of newly opening buds'. Among Multifloras, she often chose 'Thalia', 'Euphrosyne' and 'Waltham Rambler', while of Wichuraianas she says, they presented quite a new aspect of Rose beauty; preferring to trail along the ground and ramble down hill. She liked their neat, glossy foliage and in this respect Manda's trio, 'Jersey Beauty', 'Gardenia' and 'Evergreen Gem' receive special mention. Her chapter on roses for converting ugliness to beauty is full of Jekyll inspiration: for covering a painted deal summerhouse or tarred shed she suggests 'an outer skin of ramping roses' and for filling gaps in hedges she lets them 'make lovely dainty wreaths and heavy swagging garlands of their own wild will'. Displaying roses in trees delighted her and she likened it to 'painting a picture with an immensely long handled brush' as she wielded a 14 ft (4·2 m) long pole. Background for roses was important too: yew, holly, juniper, thuya or cypress would display their colours more effectively. She also liked to merge her roses into the countryside: 'The English garden I delight to dream of is also embowered in native woodland' where trees might be clothed with Ramblers above a tangle of bracken and Sweetbriar below, and to *The Rose Annual* of 1908 she contributed a piece, 'Roses in Wild Woodland'.

In her own garden Gertrude Jekyll planted wild Rugosas or hardy Scotch Briars to link her beds and borders to woodland. She used the latter associated with heathers, both thriving in her sandy, Surrey soil. These little roses had been developed in Scotland from the native *R. pimpinellifolia* (formerly *R. spinosissima*) at the end of the eighteenth century and, in a variety of colour, they gained considerable attention before longer-flowering roses became established. There are singles – pink–white 'Glory of Edzell' and bright red 'Single Cherry', 'William III' is a deep crimson semi-double – but I prefer the doubles, blush and white, with an abundance of little cupped flowers. They spread by suckering, making thickets of spring flowers followed by burnished, ferny autumn foliage and hips, dark and shiny – 'exaggerated blackcurrants', Gertrude Jekyll called them – and she even appreciated the warm bronze colouring of thickly prickled stems in winter. She also lists thirty-eight species with brief descriptions of the best way to use them; roses from China, India, the USA and Europe with a wide range of colour and diversity of habit.

Although the Reverend Joseph Pemberton is mainly considered in Part V for his important contribution to rose heritage, he must be included here for some remarks in his book published in 1908 when he deplored the Victorian neglect of species and considered no rose garden complete unless it contained a few wilder kinds. He describes those he considers worth growing in grass and how flowers from these once-blooming roses may be stretched from the end of

April to the beginning of August: from *R. ecae* and *R. banksiae* 'Lutea' to *R. bracteata* and *R. setigera*. He liked *R. macrophylla* planted with rhododendrons, *R. lucida* (now *R. virginiana*) mixed with other shrubs because of its beautiful autumn foliage and *R. rubrifolia* (now *R. glauca*) for plum-coloured stems and leaves in contrast to nearby greens. There was also the bonus of fruit to be reaped from species; Pemberton extols *R. rugosa* for this quality and mentions its use in covert planting, pheasants being partial to hips as large as wild crab apples.

R. rugosa typica makes an excellent hedge on poor soil, although carmine flowers and scarlet hips are not for confined gardens.

This handsome species was also praised by another author of Edwardian times and with some foresight she stated that the future of Rugosas was bound to be important and 'so far we have not in the least realized what its effect may be'. One of their new hybrids, 'Conrad F. Meyer', was a favourite rose of the daughter of Charles Kingsley, himself an enthusiastic rosarian; in her book *Roses and Rose Growing* (London, 1908), Rose Kingsley laments the disappearance of Hybrid Perpetuals grown at their Hampshire home, believes a rose garden without Tea Roses would not be a garden at all and considers every group in detail. However, here I just take her views on the new Ramblers, of which she gives an authoritative account, listing fully the main introductions from all countries since 1893 and drawing attention to the fact that the Wichuraianas flower late in the season, just as the Multifloras are over. She considers a 7 ft (2 m) tall weeping standard of 'Dorothy Perkins' or 'Hiawatha' to be one of the most beautiful of rose sights and draws attention to a 'Crimson Rambler' trained into a balloon shape at the Royal Gardens, Windsor, and figured in *The Garden*, 3 December 1905. She was in close touch with growers in Luxembourg and refers back to a 1907 introduction when 'a rich feast was provided for those who delight in Ramblers' with Soupert et Notting's fine new 'Bar-le-Duc', offspring of 'Souvenir de Pierre Notting' and 'Crimson Rambler', and anticipates another success with 'Bordeaux', a seedling from 'Crimson Rambler' and the dwarf Polyantha 'Blanche Rabatel'.

The majority of illustrations in *Roses and Rose Growing* are in colour and the author acknowledges help from William Paul at Waltham Cross and Henry Nicholson of New Barnet in providing specimen flowers (not for show, just ordinary garden blooms) for the plates, produced by Swain and Son at Barnet through their new process of colour printing. After the Jekyll monochrome pictures of rather distant rambler decoration in the garden, it is rewarding to find here 'Dorothy Perkins', 'Jersey Beauty' and 'Blush Rambler' in good close-up colour reproduction.

There was some affinity between the two ladies: both stressed their enjoyment of roses for the garden rather than for exhibition, but realized some guidance was necessary for the latter and obtained appropriate chapters in their books from officials of the National Rose Society: Vice-President the Rev. F. Page Roberts, a friend of Rose Kingsley, and Secretary, Edward Mawley, acknowledged by Gertrude Jekyll as an experienced rosarian.

Many Jekyll rose gardens have been restored to her original design and Mr and Mrs John Wallinger of The Manor House, Upton Grey, near Basingstoke, Hampshire, have recently executed theirs with meticulous exactitude. However, I found it even more exciting to be shown her plan for a wild garden on the other side of the house and to decipher 'Euphrosyne' among the roses suggested for planting there. With *R. arvensis*, 'Blush Rambler', 'Dundee

Rambler', 'Dorothy Perkins' and 'Jersey Beauty' – a delightful international assembly – all being given a free rein, here before long will be the kind of garden Gertrude Jekyll cherished; one to demonstrate her maxim of roses being beautifully used in natural surroundings.

CHAPTER 11

A Decorative Detour

A Victorian who looked ahead to the more artistic use of roses, Shirley Hibberd, was editor of *The Floral World* from 1858 and of *The Gardeners Magazine* from 1861. He was also author of *The Amateur's Rose Book* (London, 1894) and in a chapter on roses for decorations he drew attention to the effect of gaslight on certain colours. This important aspect had to be considered when arrangements were created by day for evening functions; carmine and crimson, he pointed out, were enhanced by artificial lighting, while purple turned muddy; white and blush showed up better in light colour schemes than buff and yellow. Here, of course, he was only considering large bloomed roses and specifically mentions Hybrid Perpetual 'American Beauty' and Hybrid Tea 'Mrs W. C. Whitney' as good cut roses, but I cannot help feeling how delighted he would have been with the scope offered by the Ramblers had he not died in 1890, before their hey-day.

Hibberd describes in detail the culture of roses in pots, forced for exhibition as well as for use in conservatory, house and even garden decoration. I always smile when I remember his description of having some ready to place in 'a little bijou plunge ground in a sheltered nook near a window' when 'potted tulips, hyacinths and alyssum have had their day'. Container grown roses – and above all Ramblers – were about to play an important part in the work of Edwardian florists, foremost among whom was R. F. Felton, whose book *British Floral Decoration* (London, 1910) has an interesting section devoted to roses. For formal work he still used some Hybrid Perpetuals ('Général Jacqueminot', 'Ulrich Brunner' and 'Mrs John Laing') but was inclining towards exciting new shades of the Hybrid Teas. As his book's frontispiece he showed a bouquet he had made for the Princess of Wales using 'Madame Abel Chatenay', from Pernet-Duchet in 1894, described as a bright carmine rose with pale vermilion and salmon tints. He considered 'La France' commendable, adding the proviso 'when good', found 'Florence Pemberton', a creamy white-suffused pink from Dickson in 1903 to be a fine all-round rose, but judged his 'Irish Elegance' of two years later, the single Hybrid Tea with orange, scarlet and apricot shading, as one of the most beautiful roses ever raised. Of the Chinas, he thought 'Queen Mab' easily the best and found Polyanthas 'sweetly pretty little pot roses'.

Ramblers took precedence in his commissions for important occasions and he must have had an enormous selection in pots for ready use. At this time it was fashionable to train their long flexible stems into all manners of shapes, the laterals cut short to maintain an outline later to be completely covered with flowers. An astonishing collection of hearts, stars, guns, windmills, airships, elephants and bridges were 'much esteemed by some of the great market men [who] grow Dorothy Perkins and cognate varieties into many singular and beautiful shapes in pots and baskets' (W. P. Wright, *Roses and Rose Gardens*, London, 1911). Although Felton recognized that such novelties might appeal to some, he preferred to use these roses classically, draping them in a natural rather than contrived fashion. He quoted the skill of the Japanese in this and transformed Claridges into a veritable bower of roses to greet royal visitors from Japan in 1890, ranging Ramblers from small standards on tables to lofty growths reaching the ceiling. Another illustration of the Royal Box at Olympia shows Their Majesties almost completely obliterated by pink roses swathed and draped in abundance while for a garden party at Marlborough House, a pavilion is festooned with equal extravagance.

Table decoration in vogue in Edwardian times; a small fountain playing amongst roses

Felton was firm in his decree that a table decoration, vase or, indeed, any arrangement of roses, should be of one colour only and, if possible, of one variety to stress an individual quality rather than, for example, mixing 'Richmond' and 'Liberty' two red Hybrid Teas, when the outline of both would be lost. He shows one of his arrangements: 'A little diplomatic dinner table, entirely dressed with Lady Gay', although I feel that serious discussion might have been impeded by such floriferous distraction completely covering the table and extending to the ceiling in an elaborate stand. This rose seems to have been one of his favourites, with flowers larger and deeper than 'Dorothy Perkins'. Others he particularly mentions are 'Gardenia' as pick of the yellows, 'Philadelphia' as a better red than 'Crimson Rambler' for pot work and 'White Dorothy' and 'François Juranville' for paler schemes. He emphasized an additional bonus from Ramblers, their splendid foliage, and advised growing a few – 'Albéric Barbier', for example – for this purpose alone. He believed 'nothing spoiled the lines of a Rose-table so completely as smilax, asparagus or other trailing foliages or ferns' and considered delicate sprays of the Wichuraianas would bring lightness to a Hybrid Tea arrangement for a large table or to Polyanthas for a smaller one.

A leading ladies' journal of 1903 illustrated a novelty of the season in floral decoration: a pair of delicate curtains composed entirely of roses and smilax, as most suitable for a drawing-room concert. Five years later, it stated that undoubtedly the most popular flower of the moment was the climbing variety of rose, especially some of the delightful pink shades of 'Lady Gay' or 'Cant's Blush' ('Blush Rambler') which 'to judge by the number of smart society functions at which these roses have been used, seem easily the first favourites'. An article of 1910 claimed that 'some of the smartest designs for floral table decoration this season require the use of artistic, miniature fountains to play automatically for several hours'. These could be hired from florists and it was suggested an arrangement might be carried out using 'Crimson Rambler', or with two shades of pink, 'Dorothy Perkins' and 'Lady Gay' and with 'little branches of these two creeping Roses straying over the edge of the fountain and trailing carelessly on the cloth to provide a deliciously refreshing scene'.

New Ramblers were
grown in pots and
trained as shields for
wall decoration.

An article in the *Gardeners' Magazine*, Vol. 51, 1908, *Rambling Roses for Decorations*, commented on their value being fully recognized by the leading floral decorators of London and 'as a consequence their cultivation has assumed considerable proportions in some of the principal market growing establishments'. As well as use for pillars, standards, and formal cylindrical specimens, here they are advocated for the embellishment of indoor apartments trained in the form of a shield. They were kept nearly flat on one side and manipulated to produce their flowers on the other, in this way occupying little space and proving more useful for positions where pillars and standards could not be used: in narrow corridors, on pedestals, on the landings of the principal staircase and, for a most splendid effect, on strong brackets round the walls of a ballroom. Again the ubiquitous pinks, 'Dorothy Perkins' and 'Lady Gay', were advocated with their drooping habit and flowers 'of a colour that appears to advantage in artificial light'.

Changes of rose fashion were reflected in millinery. In 1882 a delicate Tea Rose had been considered suitable for the demure gossamer lace afternoon cap, with perhaps another at the bosom. By the end of the century a neat coarse chip hat with a few blooms of 'La France' and white ostrich plumes and a fancy straw bonnet adorned with Banksian Roses, were fairly restrained. But in 1910, as if to echo the new bouffant Ramblers, we find a leading Oxford Street milliner advertising a hat 'combining the essentials of dressiness and usefulness . . . almost on toque lines, trimmed with a quantity of brown tulle and a wreath of natural climbing roses, with which are mingled a few moss-rose buds, furnishing a most artistic completing touch'. 'La France' was undoubtedly a very fashionable rose, lending its name to material colour as shown in a picture in 1897 of 'a gown in La France pink Duchesse, with train of pale biscuit Duchesse, adorned with La France roses'.

Development of the rose bouquet was well described by T. G. W. Henslow in *The Rose Encyclopaedia* (London, 1922) and, although a little out of context here, he goes back a century before and warrants quotation.

> When we think of the early Victorian bouquet, made in close cauliflower shape, surrounded with its white paper frill, we sigh for poor Roses wedged in with other flowers, throttled and decked out like a ham bone. But it was the spirit of the age, for even ladies tight-laced, wore crinolines, frills and sun bonnets. The style of clothing reflected itself in the bouquet; indeed, a pretty face in a sun bonnet will for ever remind me of the Victorian bouquet and its contemporary buttonhole. The age gradually became less prim, Queen Rosa smiled from the shower bouquet, with its trails of smilax and fern; the blooms were arranged in looser fashion, and bud and full-blown flower took their place amidst portions of natural foliage. Then came the American innovation of ribbon, and the bouquet was done up with trails of very narrow ribbons with flowers fastened on to the same. This style was of short duration and it soon gave way to the sheaf which is popular today . . . long stemmed flowers tied in a natural bunch with ribbons to match. The florist sighs, but the Rose grower rejoices . . .

Henslow enlarges on roses for buttonholes stressing how they are dictated by dress: for dining, a discreet Polyantha and for an overcoat by day, a large, shapely bud, preferably of a Hybrid Tea, or favoured Moss Rose.

In considering roses for exhibition, I had hoped to be able to compare the weather of 1908 with the lamentable conditions of twenty years earlier. However, apart from very hard frost and late snow in April, resulting in necessary cutting back and a preponderance of defiant suckers, and three weeks of heat and drought with very dry atmosphere even at night causing foliage as well as blooms to flag in June, I could find no evidence of either undue concern or favourable comment on climatic conditions in garden journals of the year. All were full of praise for the new decorative roses, almost to the exclusion of other types.

Reporting on the new Wichuraiana or Rambler Roses, *The Gardeners' Chronicle* said that at least thirty varieties had been introduced in the last six or seven years and as well as mentioning the established favourites, a single red, 'Stella', soft pink 'Paradise' and deep rose 'Babette' were included. Older varieties like 'The Garland' and 'Wallflower' (a vigorous Polyantha) were quite as beautiful as the modern kinds and cheaper to produce. A further article on weeping standards emphasized that it was important to choose those listed as 'evergreen wichuraianas' because 'Ramblers' (i.e. Multifloras) were not so suitable, being of coarse and rigid growth. 'Paul Transon', with exceptionally long-lasting foliage, was considered one of the best.

In a piece on the Wichuraianas, the *Journal of Horticulture* claimed the class as one coming more and more into favour, popularity being largely due to 'the spread of taste for informal gardening' and their quality of 'lending themselves perfectly to the picturesque side'. By the end of 1905 fifty-four varieties were in commerce of which three were given special mention: 'Pink Roamer', a single pink with a white centre did well in shade; pale yellow 'Jersey Beauty' was one of the best for a pillar or pergola; and 'François Foucard' gained praise for its exceptionally beautiful lemon shade. Here there was detailed comment on the Royal Horticultural Society Show at the Temple and it was emphasized that Ramblers were prominent on all the rose stands. Cants of Colchester had trained theirs, including 'The Garland' up to the roof of the tent; Prince of Oxford and Cannell of Swanley were commended for 'models of excellence'. Cutbush of Highgate had tall, arching plants of 'Hiawatha' over dwarf bushes of 'Baby Dorothy', 'Mrs W. H. Cutbush' and 'Mrs F. W. Flight', with 'Paradise' in pyramidal mounds, 'the whole scene a picture in rich pink and crimson against a background of tall palms'. From a decorative view, Paul's stand surpassed all previous efforts, but the best display, to the surprise of some, was judged to be from Hobbies of East Dereham in Norfolk, with their grand exhibit of tall standards, 'splendidly done', of 'Hiawatha', 'Minnehaha', 'Tausendschön', 'Delight' and 'Dorothy Perkins' in front of miniature standards with a few exhibition varieties to complete the display.

Comparison of roses exhibited at International Horticultural Exhibitions of 1866 and 1912 shows that of those evident at the first only two appeared at the second, when forty-four new Climbers and Ramblers took precedence and the journals of May and June were full of praise. A great many were displayed in pots and *The Gardeners' Chronicle* pointed out that 'A specimen rose used to be a large stiffly trained bush with the flowers carefully tied an equal distance apart, suggesting almonds in a pudding. How very different are the graceful airy examples that may be seen in the great tent at Chelsea today.' Charles Turner, the promoter of 'Crimson Rambler', displayed container roses for

Pink Tea Rose,
'La France' lavishly used
on wedding gown and
straw hat, 1897

Unique foliage of *R. glauca* is sought for floral
decoration and shining mahogany hips add to value
of display at Wisley.

LEFT   Striking autumn backcloth provided by
foliage and hips of *R. helenae* with contrasting
purple prunus and grey eucalyptus.

Natural climbing roses and a few Moss Rose buds were used to decorate a hat described in *The Queen*, May 1910.

conservatories, Paul's weeping standards were superb, Cutbush's Polyanthas eminently suitable for pots and Notcutts had them all in their beautiful decorative rose garden.

In a long article on 'Wichuraiana Hybrids' (*Rose Annual*, 1909) Dr A. H. Williams draws attention to the overall long flowering season; he had picked 'Gardenia' on 1 June and 'Dorothy Perkins' on Christmas Day and made a note of sixteen varieties flowering on the first day of October. Their use not only as decorative plants in the garden but as pot plants and even cut flowers is emphasized and he is the only person I have come across to mention, as well as their graceful beauty, their lasting property in water and their excellence in the bud state for buttonholes. Looking ahead to the future, he says what is wanted is varieties with autumn floriferousness of the Chinas, more fixed colours in yellow and coppery tints, crimsons and scarlets and any fresh break that is beautiful and distinct. A list of true Wichuraiana Hybrids is appended and this totals eighty-eight – a significant increase within a decade.

Thus, the Multiflora Ramblers became rather overshadowed by the decorative Wichuraianas, but I think today they hold an equally important place in our gardens and, unlike Felton, I think contrasting associations, like 'Blush Rambler' and 'Violette' in my garden, rewarding. There is a new and beautiful arrangement at Mottisfont of 'Débutante', an early pink Wichuraiana from Walsh in the USA, with 'Bleu Magenta', one of the deepest purples and the latter is used again with 'Mary Wallace', a more recent pink Wichuraiana from van Fleet, in an attractive small rose garden designed by Graham Thomas at Shugborough, a National Trust property in Staffordshire. Roses are arranged in many charming pictures in a private garden, Pyramids, South Harting, Sussex; 'Rose-Marie Viaud' mingling soft lilac with pink of 'Apple Blossom' on a little pergola, for instance.

All the pinks and purples may not, however, be right for some gardens and a subtle union of yellow, salmon and copper shades could be achieved with 'Phyllis Bide' and 'Paul Transon'. Both repeat in autumn, a rare rambling attribute. For an orange/yellow/cream concept, 'Goldfinch', would integrate happily with its hybrid 'Ghislaine de Feligonde' and, moderate growers, they could be accommodated in space unsuitable for more vigorous Ramblers. 'Sanders' White' and deep rose-pink 'Ritter von Barmstede' may be seen on the pergola of The Gardens of the Rose, near St Albans, where recently a new rose pillar/rope walk has been made near the extensive collection of old roses assembled by the Royal National Rose Society.

Roses on ropes are used in Queen Mary's Garden in Regent's Park, London and this Jekyll-favoured concept brings a decorative touch to formal planting of roses in the beds they surround. At Wisley too, garden of the Royal Horticultural Society now conveniently just off the M25, pillars and ropes of roses form decoration in the main rose planting. On all these will be found old favoured Ramblers. A typical Edwardian rose garden at Polesden Lacey, near Dorking in Surrey, is best seen at the middle of July when Ramblers on pergolas dissecting beds of roses are at their peak. Recently a splendid rose garden has been recreated by Paul Edwards at Warwick Castle, where the Countess, wife of the 5th Earl, a great gardener, grew many around the beginning of this century. This was designed by Robert Marnock in 1868 and the original plans have been used, not only for the garden, but for all the

R. mulligani (formally *R. longicuspis*) above and 'Una' below; used on ropes in Queen Mary's Garden, Regents Park, London, created in 1932.

ironwork supporting decorative roses, which include 'The Garland', 'Alberic Barbier', 'May Queen' and 'Débutante', as well as earlier *R. sempervirens* varieties. Shapely beds display representatives of all the old roses, those of Victorian times and even a new English Rose, 'Warwick Castle' from David Austin, to commemorate this authentic reconstruction. With them, standards of 'De Meaux' and 'Félicité Perpétue' contribute a further decorative aspect. The garden is open to visitors to the Castle every day from April to October.

From time to time writers have mentioned the decorative value of roses apart from their flowers. In the seventeenth century John Parkinson considered the greatest beauty of *R. villosa* was in the 'graceful aspect of the red apples, or fruit, hanging upon the bushes'. In the eighteenth Philip Miller drew attention to the smooth purple bark on young branches of *R. viriginana* and the lucid green foliage of *R. sempervirens* for 'a goodly appearance in winter'. At the beginning of the nineteenth many authors were stressing the value of rose foliage and fruit for further interest, extending rose decoration of the garden beyond the time of blooms.

CHAPTER 12

Some European Rose Gardens

THIS chapter includes visits to France and Switzerland a few years back to seek out some early twentieth century rose gardens, but any account of rose history in France would come in for criticism if it did not include some mention of the introducers of outstanding modern roses. The first recognized offspring from the hitherto dominating Hybrid Perpetuals and Teas came from Guillot of Lyon with his Hybrid Tea 'La France' in 1867 and from his nursery, too, came 'Pacquerette', the first of the

'Princess Louise', a *R. sempervirens* Rambler, 1829, decorates a pedestal at Roseraie de l'Haÿ.

Polyanthas, a class leading ultimately to Floribundas. An equally valuable contribution from the same area came with Pernet-Ducher's work to produce a true deep shade of yellow, eventually achieved by using one of his own seedlings 'Antoine Ducher' and the older 'Persian Yellow'. This he exhibited as 'Soleil d'Or' at Lyon in 1898, causing a sensation then and leading the way for many brilliant orange and flame roses in the future. In 1906 fulsome praise came from the catalogue of Thomas Henderson in New York, as, apparently, a hardy yellow rose for the northern states had been sought for many years: 'The colour of the fully expanded flower is gloriously superb: Turneresque in blending of reddish-gold, orange-yellow, nasturtium-red and opaline-pink – words are inadequate.' But surely optimum acclaim will always be accorded to Meilland (again from near Lyon, *'le berceau de la rose'*) for the introduction of 'Peace' in 1945, a story told by Antonia Ridge in *For Love of a Rose* (Faber & Faber, 1965). Revealing more about great rose breeders of the last hundred years, Jack Harkness has made an appealing assessment of their achievements in *Makers of Heavenly Roses* (Souvenir Press, 1985).

Roseraie de l'Haÿ, one of the most beautiful rose gardens in the world, grew from the enthusiasm of Jules Gravereaux, a founder of the celebrated Bon Marché chain of stores. He corresponded with and collected from all great rosarians of his time and in 1899 called in an experienced landscape architect, Edouard André, to design a garden on land adjoining the Parc de Sceaux to the south-west of Paris. By the following year, the garden's first catalogue listed a collection of 3000 roses, soon to be increased by those collected on travels through Europe, Asia and the Middle East, where Gravereaux extended his knowledge of their early history and use in perfume.

In 1906 he wrote *L'Histoire Anciénne des Roses*, tracing their development from earliest known species to roses of his time and in that year he gathered together two collections of those known to have been grown by the Empress Joséphine. One was replanted in her long-neglected garden at Malmaison, the other established at his own, where it may be seen today. After his death in 1916, his widow and family carried on with his work until 1937, when the entire property was bought by the State and is today administered by the Département du Val de Marne. The original layout has been maintained; roses are shown historically and decoratively and leading new varieties from the European trials are also displayed. It is open from 10.00 to 18.00 h from June until the end of September.

This was the garden I reached in great anticipation as early as possible one Sunday morning at the beginning of June – the roses there come earlier than in England. It covers about five acres (two hectares), tall trees form perimeter background and it is completely filled with roses, no other plants detract from the magnificent show. The summer-flowerers were past their best, but all others were splendid, particularly the Ramblers displayed in every conceivable manner: twining in trellis, draping from pedestal, arching over pergola, forming a plump or weeping standard and standing as sentinel pillar. Some of the Victorian roses were bent downwards or cupped upwards to form beautiful surrounds to borders, while more recent varieties were massed in orderly precision. As the guide book says, 'le tout forme un ensemble unique qui constitute vraiment l'apothéose de la Rose'.

A long border illustrating its history is valuable botanically with all kinds

Pergola swathed with
Ramblers gives shade at
Roseraie de l'Haÿ.

LEFT
'Mrs. F. W. Flight', an
English Rambler, well
trained as pillars at
Roseraie de l'Haÿ.

represented from species to moderns. Another section shows roses from the Orient, so important to breeders in ultimate achievements. The collection of roses up to 1800 is presented very formally, they are clipped quite hard to form rounded little bushes with limited flowers, but good blooms show the wide range of colour from dark purple 'Cardinal de Richelieu' to blush 'Rose des Peintres'. Nearby is the Malmaison border with more abandoned planting and I recollect a few lingering blooms of the old Centifolia, 'Village Maid', creamy and laced with pink. Planned to attract rose growers is the horticultural collection where hundreds of roses raised between 1850 and 1950 are displayed, many of them now lost to the trade. Two other sections have been made as a gesture to rose breeders at home and abroad; near the entrance to the garden the most successful varieties produced in France over recent years are charmingly shown around an ornamental 'Temple of Love' and the '*roses étrangères*' are grouped between this display and the main, dramatic section. Here massed beds of Hybrid Perpetuals, Hybrid Teas and Floribundas are mirrored in a pool, flanked by pergola and pillar, backed by treillage, the whole providing a remarkable scene.

Finally there are two appealing presentations; one called La Roseraie Décorative, displaying mostly modern roses, bedded and climbing, their colours carefully blended, and the other, La Roseraie de Madame, with blooms for cutting and use in bouquets and *boutonnières* – a garden for florists. Still more are to be found in the park behind this last collection, where larger shrub roses have space to show their form, and on the edge of the garden is a little open air theatre where the rose gains praise from song, dance and drama.

The Rose Garden is a comparatively recent addition to the grounds of Bagatelle, a small palace built in 1777 by the Comte d'Artois, younger brother of the King, for whom Thomas Blaikie, a Scottish landscape gardener, created the popular rustic scene. Later it was used by Napoleon as a shooting lodge and finally bought in 1838 by an Englishman, Lord Seymour, Marquis of Hertford, a friend of Napoléon III, whose small son took riding lessons in the grounds, watched by the Empress from a small kiosk, now surrounded by roses. At the beginning of this century J. C. N. Forestier, Director of Paris Parks and Gardens, thought that 'Bagatelle, quite apart from its situation in the Bois de Bologne, is unique historically . . . by restoring it and planting it afresh, we could assemble there collections of flowers . . . a rose garden . . . a living example of garden evolution.' I quote this so that visitors may realize that there is much to see, but it is generally considered that the Rose Garden is the chief glory of Bagatelle.

Work on it commenced in 1903, was completed three years later, and in 1907 the famous International Rose Trials were inaugurated by Jules Gravereaux and J. C. N. Forestier. Roses entered for the Bagatelle Trials are considered in utmost secrecy and prize-winners are planted in a place of honour near the Orangerie. I appreciate that these are indeed roses of distinction, but the purpose of my visit to these two great rose gardens created in Edwardian times was to look for contemporary roses. Although smaller than Roseraie de l'Haÿ, Bagatelle's Rose Garden seems spacious, with wide gravel walks, large areas of grass and open views to the Orangerie and kiosk, backed by many magnificent old trees. There is, of course, a large proportion of bedded modern roses – I noted 'Elizabeth of Glamis' in abundance – but this

'L'aprez-midi at Bagatelle' illustration from *The Queen*, July 1914 showing fashion in the famous rose garden.

is relieved by relaxed treatment of Ramblers and Climbers decorating the garden throughout. Pergolas lead from areas surrounded by roses on pillars connected by more on ropes; weeping standards add another dimension and lesser, rotund examples bring height to some bedded roses. Low box hedges and conifers, particularly dark green pyramids of yew, emphasize rose brilliance and some old and species roses are planted to billow naturally in grass.

At l'Haÿ the dominating Rambler was 'Alexandre Girault', completely covering the vast treillage backing the central section and pouring from a great height its floriferous deep coppery-pink clusters. 'Ghislaine de Féligonde' filled recessed alcoves below and this Rambler, inclining to orange and unknown to me, seemed most attractive. Immaculate pillars of two from England, 'Mrs F. W. Flight' and 'Paul's Scarlet', alternating pink and red, flanked the paths; on pergolas 'American Pillar' was prominent, while in the decorative section I found lovely 'Bleu Magenta' well integrated in a purple colour scheme. 'Albertine' seemed most favoured for pergolas at Bagatelle and there the weeping standards were superb, particularly 'Alberic Barbier' spilling pale yellow bloom against very dark Wichuraiana foliage. 'Auguste Gervais' glowed against yew background and 'City of York', a later descendant of 'Dorothy Perkins' from Germany, festooned ropes admirably. In both gardens I noticed 'New Dawn', sport of American 'Dr W. van Fleet', as a widely used rose for pillar, standard and climber. This dozen represents but a few of the ebullient Ramblers so well arranged to relieve more formal planting in both gardens. They brought a certain lightness and gaiety to the scene and I shall always associate them with two perfect early June days in the great rose gardens of Paris.

Coppery-red 'Alexandre Girault' makes a most spectacular display on treillage at Roseraie de l'Haÿ.

Lyon is probably the French city most associated with roses, and the Roseraie Internationale de Lyon in the Parc de la Tête d'Or is another famous garden. Towards the middle of the nineteenth century the park was landscaped in the English fashion, with vistas across grass to grouped trees and a lovely lake. In this setting a rose garden was created in 1964, one very different from the concentrated planting in Paris. Here roses are integrated with the existing landscape in three main concepts. An architectural theme dominates the centre, with a pool, pergola and paved area and most roses are planted in beds with a vista leading down to the lake. To the north there is more extensive irregular planting, well integrated with trees and the countryside, terminating with a semi-circular sweep of roses to restore the reality of a planned rose garden. The southern part has a little wandering stream and rustic bridge with roses decoratively arranged along the banks, leading to a further pool and cascade. Many small rambler standards were again planted to give height to the beds and some beautiful examples of weepers stood alone as sculptures: 'Paul Noël', almost a perfect sphere and 'Albertine' flowing to the ground. On a sloping bank miniature roses had been massed with tiny campanula and viola to form a magic carpet of colour. Interest is maintained throughout the year by careful choice of perennials, flowering shrubs and bulbs to provide some colour in every month and when the large deciduous backing trees have lost their foliage, greenery is supplied by conifers of varied shape and colour. This is indeed an immense garden of roses rather than a traditional rose garden, one of which Gertrude Jekyll would have approved and I was reminded of her insistence on imaginative merging with the countryside. A new collection of historic roses was being assembled at the Lyon Botanic Garden nearby, the plants small at the time, but I am sure this would be well worth seeing now.

Although the famous Meilland establishment was transferred from the Lyon area to the Cap d'Antibes in the 1940s, the name, Richardier-Meilland, is still found at Tassin-la-Demi-Lune to the west of the city; I was taken to this birthplace of so many famous roses and saw those named for the family blooming brilliantly. I see from the catalogue that the favourite old Ramblers are still supplied: weeping standards of 'Dorothy Perkins', 'White Dorothy', red 'Excelsa' and 'Paul Noël', the perfect one I had seen in the Lyon Garden, of 'Peace' shades, but not available in England.

I had been taken to Lyon by a friend who lives in Geneva and was disappointed that the roses in her city's Parc de la Grange were not yet properly out. I fear I cannot do justice to the rose garden by the lake with its small viewing building overlooking a series of pools, terraced on different levels with spacious rose planting on either side and reminiscent of Mogul gardens in Kashmir. In a more informal area, species grow in grass and *R. foetida* 'Bicolor' was making an eye-catching group – a rose not often planted in public places. Both this Swiss rose garden and that at Lyon are important in the staging of national and international rose trials.

Richard Huber is famed as an important rose grower and, like Rivers of Sawbridgeworth, his nursery was once renowned for fruit trees. At Dottinkon, south of Zurich, they began to specialize in older varieties of roses in 1960, not yet out when I was there at the beginning of June. However, my visit coincided with the first flush of shrub roses and I have never seen them better displayed than they are by Huber, against every form and colour of conifer,

RIGHT
'Albertine'
weeps to the ground at
Parc de la Tete d'Or,
Lyon.

110

'Tausendschõn'
(Germany 1906) grows
well in Parc de la
Grange, Geneva today.

which also provide protection. Rugosa hybrids are tolerant of cool conditions and 'Agnes' from Canada was grown as a pillar, lemon flowers well shown against dark green foliage and pink 'Sarah van Fleet' from America grown in the same way. 'Marguerite Hilling', pink sport of 'Nevada' had a glaucous cedar as foil, but almost breathtaking was the display of Kordes hybrids of *R. pimpinellifolia*. I have never seen them grown to such proportions: up through the evergreens and falling in great cascades of bloom. 'Frühlingsgold', 'Frühlingsmorgen', 'Frühlingsduft' were there, but the most spectacular were 'Frühlingszauber' deep pink against blue conifer and 'Frühlingsfang', white pouring through darkest green. These are the Huber roses I will always remember and again I was reminded of Gertrude Jekyll's wise words on conifer background.

I have recently corresponded with a Swedish rose expert, Göte Haglund, who has played an important part in the creation of a new Rosarium in Gothenburg, the city founded by King Gustavus Adolphus II in 1524, with parkland to be preserved for posterity. According to Göte Haglund in *The Rose, Queen of Flowers* (Gothenburg, 1987) this was landscaped in the English fashion in the 1890s as at Lyon, and the Rosarium has been set in part of the park of the Horticultural Society, now belonging to the City of Gothenburg. The book traces the history of roses and the information is intended to supplement planting in the Rosarium, where roses are to be found in appropriate sequence from earliest to modern. In introductory acknowledgement the author tells of obtaining old roses from Denmark, France, Germany and England and of his travels to collect further information from some of the same sources as I did. I note that an attempt is to be made to collect all known China and Tea Roses for growth in the subtropical greenhouse; already they have come from East Germany, France, England and the USA, while it is hoped to obtain some from Australia. It is truly a rose garden of shared heritage and demonstrates Sweden's interest in the history and conservation of roses.

Part V

Introduction, an Indian Interlude and Restoration

A rose does not preach – it simply spreads its fragrance

MAHATMA GANDHIJI

'Cornelia'

CHAPTER 13

Roses from Havering-atte-Bower

THE name of this Essex village seems to suggest flowers of long ago and, in fact, there is an historic rose connection, with two royal residences situated there: The Bower, hunting-box of kings and Pyrgo Palace, dower house of queens. When Yorkist Edward IV married Elizabeth, widow of Lancastrian Sir John Grey, as a mark of allegiance every year at midsummer she had to present the King with a white rose, presumably gathered at Pyrgo Palace. This story is recounted by The Reverend Joseph Pemberton in his book, *Roses, their History and Cultivation* (London, 1908) as he also lived and grew his roses at Havering-atte-Bower. In the Introduction he looks back to his early life, remembering being brought up in 'an atmosphere of roses', and taken by his father to the Crystal Palace shows where orders were placed with Rivers. On Sundays he wore – in competition with considerably more adult church-goers – a rose in the buttonhole of his Norfolk jacket and cherished a bud of 'Souvenir de la Malmaison' over a whole term at boarding school. He learned to bud when he was twelve and had his own roses; three red standards which did not do well in the small, shady situation allotted to him. However he remembered splendid examples in the main rose beds and borders of the kitchen garden: 'La Reine', 'Madame Laffay', 'Général Jacqueminot' and 'Salet' among them and, in odd places, thrust aside to make room for their more fashionable successors, older 'Maiden's Blush', 'Old Cabbage', 'Tuscany' and 'Common Moss'. Although Joseph Pemberton Senior was an accomplished grower of roses, he did not show them and in 1874, the year after his death, the first Pemberton roses appeared at the Crystal Palace to win a second prize to spur his son to gain major awards every year. In 1896, for instance, he showed roses on forty-nine occasions from mid-June until the first week in August and took forty-eight prizes. He was the first recipient of the Dean Hole Medal in 1909, became President of the National Rose Society (1911–13), and later gained many awards as a hybridest.

For some time he had been a vicar in Romford and lived, with his sister Florence, at the Round House in Havering, an imposing eighteenth-century dwelling built on one of the highest points in the county by a tea merchant, so that he could view his clippers sailing up the Thames. Florence was an equally enthusiastic rosarian and there they founded a nursery, proclaiming on the cover of the 1913 catalogue: 'We appreciate a visit from the lovers of roses, whether purchasers or not ... it is a pleasure to have a talk ...' *The Garden* of 14 March 1908 had given the Pemberton book a long review, being critical of a section covering species, praising Miss Pemberton's illustrations on budding, etc., and thoroughly recommending it to rose lovers and gardeners for the 'unexpected character of its contents'. *The Rose Annual* (1908) carried a review by Mr E. P. Linsell, President of the National Rose Society, who did not agree with the advocated methods of pruning, but again gives general acclaim: 'The Pemberton name, a household word among rosarians, as a skilful grower, successful exhibitor and unrivalled judge, will be elevated by this publication.' Two chapters on the soil and its treatment and on planting, demonstrate Pemberton's thoroughness and might well be studied by many today who cursorily plant a rose and expect it to thrive without careful preparation. A second edition was warranted twelve years later by the emergence of new roses, an increase in the prevalence of blackspot and an advance in garden chemistry. With characteristic reticence, his own 'Perpetual Flowering Musk Rose' is given scant reference in the text, but the updated Appendix of selected roses, with valuable guidance regarding their particular use in the garden, includes thirteen, seven bred at Havering.

Pemberton had first called his roses 'Hybrid Teas' and thus they were advertised in the 1916–17 catalogue with reproductions of photographs from *The Gardeners' Magazine* of 'Danae' and 'Moonlight', both earlier award winners in 1913. Special mention is also given to 'Ceres' and 'Galatea' of the following year, with 'Clytemnestra' and 'Queen Alexandra' ('named by Her Majesty's gracious permission') in 1915. A third illustration is of 'Pemberton's White Rambler', a Multiflora type with large trusses of upright stems, 'particularly useful for floral decoration'. It is said that his classification was queried at a show by one of his contemporaries, whose nose detected their outstanding fragrance: he suggested 'Hybrid Musks'. Actually this is misleading in that the link with *R. moschata* is somewhat tenuous. Pemberton had used a rose called 'Trier', a sweet-scented seedling from 'Aglaia', of *R. multiflora* and 'Rêve d'Or' parentage. The latter, a Noisette, did claim some musk ancestry, but it is more likely that the *multiflora* fragrance dominates in the Hybrid Musks. However, this outstanding quality in their clustered blooms lasting well into the autumn, their healthy foliage and strong form soon established their place among modern shrub roses.

How they carried on at the nursery after their head gardener, John Bentall, joined the army in the First World War is best described by Joseph Pemberton himself and, through the kindness of his son I am able to quote in full two letters sent to France, the first dated 10 May 1917.

Illustration from the Pemberton catalogue of 'Moonlight' (1913), winner of three gold medals and used as a hedge at Kew later.

Dear Mr. Bentall,

I was very pleased to get a letter from you and in reply will tell you something of rose prospects. There are no R.H.S. shows this year; only the fortnightly shows at the old "Drill Hall" close to Buckingham Palace. This was the place where the R.H.S. used to hold its meetings before the Horticultural Hall was built, which has now been taken over by the Government. The Drill Hall is cramped and dark; small compared with the Vincent Square Hall, but large enough so far for the exhibits which are very few. Last Tuesday, the two Cants, Hicks, Prince and Wm. Paul staged small exhibits. No new roses except one or two from Hicks. N.R.S. has given up the Spring Show in the Botanic, but they want to hold an autumn show at the Drill Hall on Sept 11th but I doubt if it will come off. The trade growers haven't any men left. George Prince told me last Tuesday he had only 3 old men and how he was to get the budding done he couldn't imagine.

I expect Mrs. Bentall has told you we got the seedling briar and laxa stocks from France just before Christmas. I had a job to find them: they had been lying at Stepney Docks for 6 weeks with the label lost. They are larger than those we had from Holland. The long winter stopped planting, but we got them all in by April 25: the ground was moist and although the weather is harsh and dry, the stocks are moving and I think the seedling briars will be good. But who is to bud them all! Red, the boy, and myself are pruning at Scotchers Clytemnestra, Q. Alexandra, as you know. It is late and some, I fear will have to be left, but all the Island and Dairy Beds are done. We have no forced roses in the 'Tucker' house this year and although we have one side filled with plants just budding up I don't expect they will be ready for fertilizing before June. There are about 300 seedlings in pots in the Tucker house, down the middle and at the far end, the left hand side being potatoes in boxes. Seedlings in boxes are in the melon ground house. The payments for the plants supplied in the autumn have come in fairly well and as soon as I have time to make out the total will hand Mrs. Bentall her percentage. Mrs. Bentall is a very great help and I do not know what I should have done without her. The boy is anxious to learn rose growing – his grandfather at Theydon Bois has 2 acres of roses – and he picked up the way to prune quickly. He is observant, but wants someone with him to hustle him a bit. As soon as the ground gets soft again the maidens must be staked; a good many already want tieing. I accepted an invitation to judge the new roses in Paris in June, but there now seems no chance of getting there this

year. I enclose a press cutting which may interest you. Don't trouble to return
it. I wish your C.O. would give you a month's leave in July to help in the
budding. If you like, shew him the paper.

Yours faithfully,

Joseph H. Pemberton.

The second was written on 7 August 1917:

Dear Mr. Bentall,

I had yr. letter of June 24th and was pleased to get it. Yes, the yellow rose, a
row at Scotchers, flowered well at the tips of the long shoots, but nowhere else:
that's the drawback and the old plants in the Dairy bed did just the same.
Unless I can find out the way to treat it, the rose will be no good to the general
public. However, Mrs. Bentall has budded 500 of it at Scotchers, so perhaps by
the year these will flower, 1919, we shall know its real value. We have a lot of
heps in the Tucker house fertilized from it. The rose for next year is 'Pax', the
white spray. We shewed a few stems of it at the R.H.S. fortnightly meeting on
July 3 and put up a pole and vases of it on July 17th R.H.S. meeting, when the
N.R.S. judged seedling roses. It got a certificate, but was really worth a gold
medal, as they will see in years to come. I am certain this rose has a future and
will be in everybody's garden. It caught the public's fancy and we have taken
addresses to let them know when it is sent out. If the War is over we will send it
out in the autumn of 1918, but it will be useless to do so while the War lasts;
there are no buyers now. We have budded 1,700 of it at Scotchers. It bids fair to
be a good autumn rose, because after cutting down the old plants for buds, it
has thrown up strong growth from the base, bearing large clusters of bud –
good heads – which will be flowering in September.

Of the seedlings budded last year there is one especially promising, a bright
red cluster, semi single with fine golden stamens. I budded 10 plants and from
these I have budded 150 at Scotchers and the autumn growth is strong, bearing
good buds. I think we can get at least another 100 buds from these few plants.

We are in a muddle for stocks for autumn and spring planting. I ordered a lot
from Orleans as last year; they have booked the order, but the export of them to
England is prohibited from anywhere and I hear they will stop all nursery stock
from coming in for at least 12 months after the War. Added to this the severe
winter killed all our cuttings and nearly everyone else's as well and until a week
ago I could not get any. Then I found that there's some at Woking and went
down to see. I got 4,000 manetti, but the price was more than double the usual
figure. I am saving some of the stocks planted for budding this year. Shall lift
them and lay in by heels until the spring in the hope they will not be too large.
We will not bud ordinary roses now, but get a few plants from the trade. I do
not expect many orders this year, so perhaps we shall tide over the difficulty.
Irish growers are just as badly off for stocks as English growers. The stocks we
are budding this year, especially the briars at Scotchers are very good, the best
we have had for years, nor more than 2 in a 100 dead. I enclose a list of Scots
budding; it may interest you. Now we are budding Meyer briars at Island. It is
a job to get through it all; only Mrs. B. and myself.

Yours faithfully

J. H. Pemberton.

The list referred to in the second letter is headed 'Scotchers Budding, 70 in a row' and it is interesting to see that 'Pax' takes up twenty-four rows, by far the most, obviously in anticipation of its launch. Scotchers was an additional 2½ acres (1 hectare) of land with good topsoil and plenty of clay beneath, situated a quarter of a mile away from the original nursery, where some 35–40,000 roses were grown annually for sale, although not all would be purchased. There were three main areas for roses near the Round House: the Dairy Bed for most of the seedlings, Hybrid Musks and Hybrid Teas occupied the Island Bed, near the pond where the young Bentall used to fish, with Ramblers and Clustered Roses (Poulsen's Type) in Butcher's Mead. 'Pax' was duly introduced in 1918 and was awarded that year a Gold Medal by the NRS, to be followed by more outstanding roses from Havering-atte-Bower in the next decade – 'Prosperity', 'Penelope' and 'Cornelia' among them. Florence Pemberton carried on for a further three years after her brother's death in 1925, bringing out the lovely silvery-pink 'Felicia' and brilliant red 'Robin Hood'. All the roses of the Pemberton Nursery were bequeathed to their gardeners, who set up their own, Bentall at Havering and Spruzen at Stapleford Abbotts.

At this point my story might have stopped, had I not gone one day to the Round House, to see if I could find any remnants of Pemberton roses there. I learned that they were being replanted in the garden, but that the person I really ought to see was Jack Bentall, just down the road. This was better fortune than I had anticipated; here was someone who had known 'The Rev' and during the last few years I have gleaned much information and pleasure from a good memory and a lively, humorous mind. The Westminster Shows meant frequent expeditions to London in the 1920s, helping to erect stands, putting the van in a nearby garage for 6d (even then parking in Horseferry Road was difficult) before young Jack could slip off to the Oval, with the approval of 'The Rev'. He could not have been a more considerate employer and was the first in the area to give his staff Saturday afternoons off for shopping. Her son remembers that his mother was given the tiniest budding knife he had ever seen and how deftly she worked with it, budding all the new seedlings and having success with 'Mermaid' (brought out by George Paul in 1917), a rose notoriously difficult to propagate and passed to the Pemberton Nursery for her expert attention.

When the Bentalls were on their own she carried on with hybridizing and it may not be appreciated that credit is due to Ann for many roses with a Bentall reference in rose records, three of which proved long-lasting with their success. In 1932, contrary to belief that it was a sport, she bred 'The Fairy' from 'Paul Crampel', a dwarf Pompom and 'Lady Gay', the Edwardian Rambler. I saw the original in Jack's garden, measuring 4 ft 6 in × 5 ft (1·3 m × 1·5 m) and still producing a quantity of the dainty pink trusses, now seen universally. The parentage of 'Ballerina' is not known; Ann discovered it as a chance seedling and foresaw its possibility, although Jack says his father never thought much of it. He believes 'William Allen Richardson' was used in the breeding of 'Buff Beauty', the Hybrid Musk, praised worldwide, but there were many others: 'Nancy' with trusses of white-eyed red flowers, pink 'Belinda', after which Jack and Maud Emma named their daughter (not the other way round as is usually the case) and dark red 'Rosaleen'. Jack

OVERLEAF BOTTOM
'Penelope', one of the most successful Pemberton Hybrid Musks and still ranking high amongst selected Shrub Roses.

OVERLEAF TOP
For a small pool in a Hampshire garden, 'The Fairy' of correct scale, makes a perfect surround.

OVERLEAF RIGHT
'Buff Beauty', one of Mrs. Bentall's popular roses, well lit by the setting sun.

discovered some papers relating to the 1930s: an order from the Earl of Buchan at Virginia Water of 1935, he thinks for planting at the golf course, of some 200 Hybrid Musks, including four dozen 'Fortuna', a soft pink awarded in 1927 a NRS Gold Medal (the trophy passed to Ann), and her yellow Hybrid Tea 'Sunray'.

A consignment note from the London & North Eastern Railway, February 1937, shows roses for Kenilworth, Painswick in Gloucestershire, Guernsey, Ipswich and Seaford – evidence of widespread demand for Bentall roses. On the cover of their 1939–40 catalogue is a picture of 'Pax' and the welcoming invitation to come and talk roses is still included. There is also an illustration of 'Moonlight' used as a hedge in Kew Gardens and among Hybrid Musks listed were 'Robin Hood', 'good for massing', 'Sammy', advocated for a hedge, and 'Thisbe', stressed for fragrance. An interesting inclusion under Climbing Roses is 'Miss Marion Manifold', a very vigorous crimson which Jack Bentall maintains came from Australia. Although it is not included in Trevor Nottle's list of Alister Clark's roses mentioned in Part III, it sounds very like one of the many he named for his friends. There is a good list of Polyanthas, including 'The Fairy': 'Splendid for bedding, free from mildew, one of the very best, new' and mention of a Certificate of Merit from the NRS.

Throughout the Second World War Jack worked at Romford, making generators for aircraft engines; his mother died in 1941, his father was not well and the nursery ran down. Afterwards he was encouraged to start up again and used to go out into the hedges and woods to collect briars – 1000 at a time – and before long he was supplying St James's Palace with roses. There was also a ready market on his doorstep with the development at Harold Hill to house many from London's East End; folk who had no experience in gardening. He would deliver over the weekend so that he could show them how best to plant roses and sometimes to investigate failures – like the time when they had been planted in bags of soot because somebody had been told it was good for them and, on another occasion, a standard 'Albertine' had been submerged 3 ft 6 in (1 m) deep, being too tall for a chosen place.

By the 1970s, when their place in gardens was assured, Jack was selling many of the best Hybrid Musks again and it is good to know that his successors, are endeavouring to collect them all for distribution in due course from Brokenbacks Nursery, Havering-atte-Bower. Jack and Emma Maud retired to Harold Wood in 1985 and I had no difficulty in finding them, with the most colourful little front garden in the area and his pretty standards fully out to welcome me. Now he is there alone, but still helping his friends to bud: 'a sitting down job' and a long way from the time some sixty-five years ago when he and young Spruzen did the budding at Scotchers, his father cutting the budwood each morning and others to tie in with bass behind them. I have his half-standards flowering in my garden now in late October; 'Prosperity', 'Felicia', 'The Fairy' and 'Ballerina' – their blooms lingering evidence of Pemberton and Bentall expertise.

Back in 1923, Joseph Pemberton had stated in *The Rose Annual* 'The time is coming when a distinct class, named Shrub Roses, will obtain official recognition', and although there was occasional reference to their informal use, it was not until thirty years later that the NRS added a table for shrub roses to its analyses in their *Annual*. Then 'Penelope', 'Cornelia' and 'Felicia' were

Jack Bentall with picture of The Rev. Joseph Pemberton, his father and a fine display of 'Ceres' in the Dairy Bed.

recognized and eight years later they were still there, with 'Prosperity', 'Vanity' and 'Wilhelm', the last from Kordes. With 'Ballerina' they continued to maintain their place, frequently starred for fragrance, and were included in later lists of roses suitable for hedges. In 1987 'Ballerina' was second only to 'Nevada' and five other roses from Havering-atte-Bower were still shown to be deservedly popular. Certainly they have fulfilled the Pemberton forecast and are today universally used as shrub roses, hedges and, given the chance, as climbers – 'Cornelia' reached 20 ft (6 m) up a mimosa in the Isle of Wight. They make substantial bushes, the majority rarely needing any support, (although 'Wilhelm' is rather lax) with splendid early foliage, often red-tinged, and dark stems, well offsetting pale blooms. It cut back to a good eye after first flowering the autumn showing can be equally rewarding and then the buds seem more brilliant than earlier in the year. Some have good hips and late flowers should be left, particularly on 'Penelope': I know of no other rose with such lovely coral-celadon fruit and I have used it with late 'Felicia' flowers for indoor decoration at Christmas. 'Ballerina' makes a shorter, compact bush, ideal for mid-border position, while 'The Fairy' will tumble in the front, or surround a small pool perfectly, as demonstrated in The Gardens of the Rose, near St Albans.

As a gesture in honour of her eightieth birthday, the National Gardens Scheme created a Queen Elizabeth the Queen Mother Rose Walk leading down from The Mall to the lake in London's St James's Park. It runs between beds of brilliant roses, but at the bottom to the right and parallel to the water is a border of more discreet Hybrid Musks, with 'Trier' included. One summer evening I paused there, when the fragrance was intense and I thought how well these pale roses of classical name, reflected their creator, himself no extrovert, as related by *The Garden* in his obituary, with emphasis on his 'unassuming knowledge, readily imparted to those who sought it, but never ostentatiously paraded'. I thought about Ann Bentall's achievements; how pleased she would have been with her 'Buff Beauty' here included, to know that roses introduced from Havering-atte-Bower had formed the basis for establishing a new class of shrub roses and that her son has contributed much to my story.

CHAPTER 14

Roses from Ram Bagh to Chandigarh

JOSEPH Pemberton, as already mentioned, appreciated the importance of wild roses and the Himalayan Musk Rose, *R. brunonii*, would surely have interested him in view of his involvement with fragrance in the Hybrid Musks. His thoughts would also have been directed eastwards by those scented garden roses of China, some come to the West via Calcutta, and to India's long association with rose perfume. When the Essex breeder was creating his new roses in the 1920s, far away others were being massed in beds and planted for pergolas in Delhi's new Government House garden. This was 400 years after Babur, first Mogul Emperor of India (1526–30) was contemplating the arid land alongside the Jumna at Agra, where he found it impractical to make the traditional Persian garden and had to compromise: 'In every corner I created suitable gardens: in every garden I planted roses and narcissi regularly and in beds corresponding to each other.' Undoubtedly Damasks would have been included as this rose had long been used for perfume and pink roses predominate in early Persian miniatures, although red, yellow and white have also been discerned. On the riverside, cool chambers were built below ground level, with platforms above, from which might be viewed the fine symmetry of this Ram Bagh – Garden of Rest. The Persian *charbagh* was a square formal garden dissected into four by crossed watercourses; these channels became wider and more imposing as time progressed. At the Ram Bagh, many narrow ones may still be traced and, of course, they provided the very necessary irrigation for roses. In 1632 an

English traveller, Peter Mundy, described the garden surrounding the tomb of a later emperor, Akbar (1556–1605) at Sikandra, as 'a square garden divided into lesser squares and that into other like bedds and plotts; in some little groves of trees ... in other squares are your flowers, herbes, etc. whereof Roses, Marigolds ...'. These flowers are consistently associated in India today in welcoming garlands and tributes.

Akbar's son, Jahangir (1605–27) and his wife, Nur Jehan, both loved flowers, preferred the hills to the plains and established many beautiful gardens in Kashmir. It is said that hundreds of them were created around Dal Lake, backed by the imposing mountains, in the first half of the seventeenth century. Jahangir himself wrote: 'Kashmir is a garden of eternal spirit ... the red rose, the violet and the narcissus grow of themselves ... there were flower carpets of fresh rosebuds ...' and of the Fath Bagh at Ahmedabad he noted, 'The plot has bloomed well, it was pleasant to see so many Red Roses, owing to their scarcity in India.' He chose to be buried in his garden at Verinag, where roses were planted either side of the wide canal, doubly impressive in reflection. This was in the hills away from Dal Lake, the source of the river Jehlum supplying all the necessary water and, not far away, another was cascaded down to feed fountains and pools in successive terraces at Achabal, favourite garden of Nur Jahan. It is said that there she had a mound covered with rose bushes, perhaps to supply the rose-water for her bath, and that one day she noticed drops of oil floating on the surface, had them skimmed off and named the sweet-scented product Attar-i-Jehangiri – the original essential oil for rose perfume. Her father, I'timad-ud-daula, was a great lover of gardens; for his tomb it was decreed 'rose bushes should border the raised walk, bending over to break the hard edges of the stonework' and many rose beds are maintained today in extensive gardens surrounding the building.

Towards the end of the eighteenth century, a botanic garden was established at Calcutta and Dr William Roxburgh, an experienced botanist and employee of the East India Company, was appointed Superintendent in 1793. He organized plant collection from all over the country and, like Reeves in China, supervised local artists employed to record them. Plants from China were also brought by ships calling in at Calcutta and were grown on at the botanic garden. In the comprehensive *Flora Indica*, (Vol. II, Calcutta, London, 1832), Roxburgh mentioned plants received from Canton, believing *R. chinensis* to be the *R. indica* of Linnaeus. *R. microphylla* (*R. roxburghii roxburghii*) the double pink as pictured in the Reeves collection, was another known in Calcutta and also *R. triphylla*, a moderate climber with small, full-clustered white flowers, later known as *R. anemoneflora*. Many beautiful species roses have come from the Himalayas; among them an invasive climber, *R. brunonii* (1823) of which the lovely large single white 'La Mortola' is a form, and *R. macrophylla* (1818), making a substantial bush with purplish foliage, bright pink blooms and a wealth of pendulous hips. *R. clinophylla*, emanating from the Calcutta Botanic Garden in 1816, is, according to Roy E. Shepherd (*History of the Rose*, New York, 1954), a white rose closely resembling *R. bracteata*, found in marshy areas of India, but is not at present in cultivation in Britain.

Information on roses arriving in India during the nineteenth century has been collected from two books covering gardening generally and shows that

R. anemoneflora, white from pinkish buds, needs a sheltered wall to climb as here provided, at Jenkyn Place, Bentley, Hampshire.

many favoured in other parts of the world maintained a place in Indian gardens, although conditions on the plains were not conducive to growth of all varieties. 'Roses look well in a parterre by themselves or a few distributed along borders' advised G. Speede in his *Indian Handbook of Gardening* (Calcutta, 1841). This has a list of eight headed by the 'Madras' or 'Rose Edouard' ('v. common, no garden without it'): a cause of some contention, there being the West-recognized rose from the Île de Bourbon of the same name. B. S. Bhatcharji, in *Rose Growing in the Tropics* (1935, 1959), wisely says no useful purpose would be served in contending whether 'Edward Rose' is of Chinese or Indian origin, but adds, 'It is an undisputable fact that for over one and a half centuries before 1769 Ittar (Essential Oil) was known and used in Delhi ... This rose should not be confused with the variety used as an understock in many parts of India and named with a peculiar spelling "Edouard".' He also points out that the name Bengal Rose is misleading, deriving from the most important province in India during early British occupation, although they were grown long before in many parts of India. He refers readers to *Bailey's Cyclopaedia of Horticulture* (1922) London, p. 2988.

Firminger's *Gardening in India* ran into many editions and in the third, of 1874, he thought few roses worthwhile, except for 'Rose Edouard', 'Common China', 'Musk' and 'Bussora', the latter a Persian rose of lovely perfume, cultivated for attar and the only Damask he knew in India. Although Speede had included Gallica and Moss in his earlier list, Firminger found them intolerant of the Indian climate and was also unable to grow Alba or Spinosissima; Sweet Briar was common, Bourbons grew well enough but produced no flowers and although Hybrid Perpetuals bloomed, they were inconsistent. In his 1894 edition Firminger remarked that in the last decade rose shows had become common in most parts of India and considered the best types for exhibition to be 'Maréchal Niel', 'Gloire de Dijon', 'La France', 'Captain Christy', 'Louis van Houtte', 'Senateur Vaisse', 'Paul Neyron' and 'Monte Christo', proving that the Hybrid Perpetuals now flourished and, indeed, he judged 'Général Jacqueminot' to be one of India's finest possessions. Among Climbers, he thought 'Devoniensis', known as 'Victoria' in gardens about Calcutta, to surpass all others.

A specific work, R. Ledlie's *Handbook of Rose Culture in India* (Calcutta, 1923) listed twenty-seven Hybrid Teas, thirteen Teas and seven Hybrid Perpetuals as the best all round varieties. Of the first, 'Florence Pemberton' (1903) and 'Dean Hole' (1904) had been bred by Dickson in Ireland, as had a number of the Teas. 'Cloth of Gold', 'La Marque' and 'Lady Hillingdon' were suitable as standards, 'Maréchal Niel' heads a short list of Climbers, including Edwardian Ramblers 'Dorothy Perkins', 'Lady Gay', 'Crimson Rambler' and 'Hiawatha'. Returning to Bhatcharji, 'Madame Isaac Pereire' appears amid the many illustrations of modern roses and his extensive list includes 'Lady Hillingdon', 'Frau Karl Druschki' and 'Cramoisi Supérieur'. Greatest acclaim is given to 'Maréchal Niel', 'the famous yellow creeper ... still reigns supreme in all tropical situations without much frost. No other climbing roses, however modern, can produce so many flowers per plant for such a length of season.'

This rose is also described as 'fabulous' by Dr B. P. Pal, FRS, in *The Rose of India* (New Delhi, 1966, 1972), also universally known for his work, particularly on wheat, at the India Agricultural Research Institute and who, in 1987, was awarded the high honour, Padma Vibhushan, for his contribution to agricultural science. There is a Dr B. P. Pal Rose Garden at the Institute, planted with roses developed in India – he himself bred over eighty – and his love of the flower goes back to the time of his youth in Burma at the beginning of this century, when he remembers growing 'Frau Karl Druschki', shell-shaped and pure white with 'Gloire de Margottin', dazzling red. His excellent book is largely taken up with India's roses of today and is packed with relevant information, but there are also many points of interest to this story.

Dr Pal considers the rose season to be 'sheer heaven' in the northern plains from the end of November to the end of March, when some may have up to four flushes of bloom. He stresses that Ramblers are the glory of hill stations in early summer, a time when hot winds blow on the plains, mentioning 'Albertine', 'Sanders White', 'Paul's Scarlet', 'American Pillar', 'Violette' and 'Veilchenblau'. Writing on the Shrub Garden, Dr Pal insists that here roses should 'possess adequate size, be well clothed with leaves and look handsome even when not in bloom' – a point rarely emphasized. Hybrid Musks are mentioned as doing well on the plains and 'Prosperity' singled out for special mention, and of the old-fashioned roses he lists 'Souvenir de la Malmaison', 'Madame Pierre Oger' and 'Madame Hardy'.

In an interesting chapter on rose-water and rose-oil, he mentions a theory that Queen Elizabeth I used Indian perfumes; and gives details of the original centres of manufacture. Dr Pal considers roses most suitable for perfume today are 'Bussora' and 'Rose Edouard', while 'Gruss an Teplitz', a crimson rose of China derivation, has been used for experimental purposes. I see the latter is given a rich, spicy fragrance by Graham Thomas, who has a most discerning nose for roses (see his *Shrub Roses of Today*, pp. 204–13).

Through an introduction from Professor William Stearn, who had known him at Cambridge, I contacted Dr Pal before I left England and was delighted to be invited, on arrival in Delhi, to see the new National Rose Garden of the Rose Society of India, of which he is an extremely active President Emeritus for life. Recently the Government has made available two plots in Chanakya-puri (Diplomatic Enclave in New Delhi); one for display, the other for trial

Dr Pal grows his roses
and bougainvillea in
pots on his high terrace
garden in New Delhi.

A fountain plays high in the Zakir Rose Garden, Chandigarh and Dr Pal's pink 'Delhi Princess' occupies the foreground.

TOP LEFT
Dr B. P. Pal recommends the 1843 Bourbon 'Souvenir de la Malmaison' for gardens on the Indian Plains.

LEFT BOTTOM
Acclaimed the world over, 'Devoniensis', English Tea Rose, was known in the Calcutta area as 'Victoria'.

A rose offering; detail
from eighteenth century
mural, City Palace,
Udaipur.

and experiment. We were joined by the Director and head gardener who
explained how roses flourish in Delhi's dry heat and, unlike those in Bombay
where humidity proves disastrous, have no black spot. On this account roses
are exported to the Gulf States with similar climate and cut blooms are
welcome in Europe in winter months. Irrigation takes place every other day
but after the monsoon rains, the labour force has to be doubled due to the
sudden appearance of vast quantities of weeds. Well-known roses from other
countries are included, but I particularly liked one of Pal breeding: warm pink
'Delhi Princess' of lovely scent and long-lasting in my hotel room. Miniatures,
Polyanthas, well-grown standards and Climbers add decoration to this
immaculate rose garden. Dr Pal took me to see his home collection and I was
surprised to find it entirely displayed in pots staged in his high terrace garden;
roses of all types and colours ranging from tiny seedlings to quite substantial
bushes, alongside many bougainvilleas, in which he also specializes, and
pansies. One of his favourite roses for pot growth is 'Echo', a Polyantha form
of 'Tausendschön', covered with pink and white blooms, a rose not available in
England today, although it was in the 1939–40 Bentall catalogue. I relished
this rewarding time with the expert whom I had hitherto only known through
his contributions to *The Rose Annual*. We still correspond and I enjoy thinking
of him, 'a bachelor wedded to roses', surrounded by his lovely collection.

As the tour proceeded from Delhi to Agra, Rajasthan and Kashmir, I made
notes for this chapter. In the Taj Mahal gardens they are grown in formal beds
alongside rectangular canals, but in an area to one side, possibly a nursery, I
found quantities of 'Old Blush China', darkened by incessant sun. Fatepur
Sikri, the city built by Akbar in 1596 and soon after abandoned to the desert,
grows no roses now, but they are preserved for ever, carved on sandstone
pillars, as they are in marble of the palaces at Amber and Deeg. Fountains, fed
from a Udaipur lake on a higher level, still patter on large leaves and egrets
wade in the flooded rosebeds of Saheliyon-ki-Bari, the garden of a princess
who loved to hear the sound of rain. Jodhpur's Mandore Garden has quite a
substantial planting of roses, maintained by constant irrigation with water
stored underground, collected from occasional rainfall on the extensive rocky
plateau. Damasks and 'Rose Edouard' were seen growing, but their flowerheads were more often in evidence marketed in large baskets as objects for
devotion and decoration: as offerings at the entrance of the Jain Temple at
Ranakpur and their petals being constantly rearranged in wreaths of meticulous pink and marigold-orange on Gandhi's polished black marble shrine in
Delhi or carefully placed to spell out an hotel's greeting to a visiting
delegation. We were all garlanded with roses on two occasions: our coach filled
with fragrance and, by the end of the day, its floor was carpeted with petals.

At Srinagar on Dal Lake, roses were evident in the local crafts; woven in
carpets, painted on papier mâché – the only blooms to be found in Kashmir in
early April. Hard-pruned roses filled countless beds in the famous gardens
around the lake and clung to terrace walls of Nishat Bagh (Garden of
Gladness). However, I found no evidence of those described seventy years
before at Shalimar Bagh (Abode of Love), a garden made by Jahangir for Nur
Jahan: 'The loveliest roses in the garden are the Maréchal Niels, which climb
the grey–green walls of the Hall of Public Audience and hang their soft yellow
globes head downwards in clusters from the carved cedar cornice' (C. M.

Villiers-Stuart, *Gardens of the Great Moguls*, 1913). However, I was delighted to hear from a guide at Verinag that roses are to be planted so that they will overhang the hard edges of stonework bordering the broad canal, just as they did in Jahangir's time. He told me to come again, in May, the best month for roses in Kashmir.

On our final day Joy Lee and I diverted from the programmed visit to Government House gardens in Delhi and caught an early flight north, to be greeted on arrival at the airport with a large poster announcing 'Welcome to Chandigarh, City of Roses'. This was the favourite flower of Jawaharlal Nehru (he wore a different bloom each day and always expressed his admiration for them) who conceived the idea of a 'new town symbolic of the freedom of India, unfettered by the traditions of the past . . . an expression of the nation's faith in the future'. Certainly Corbusier's Chandigarh, completed in the 1960s, is in no way confined: wide streets are bordered by broad verges and an open Leisure Valley runs like a swathe of the countryside right through the city with spacious gardens devoted to certain plants. However, it has been said that 'the Zakir Rose Garden is the Kohinoor of all these gems' and this was the purpose of our visit.

It was designed by Dr M. S. Randhawa in 1966–7 and covers thirty acres with the distant Shivalik Hills as background to the north and a central fountain rising high into the sky; its very spaciousness spelling freedom. Few people were about when we arrived at 7.30 a.m. to find the roses, fresh from the cool of the night. They are widely dispersed in beds, but not necessarily in formal arrangement, and the beds themselves are distributed to integrate into the landscape and associate with flowering trees and shrubs. There are four main concepts showing the best known varieties throughout the world, those most useful for decoration, a fragrant collection with high oil content and, finally, one of roses used for research. An ultimate collection of 60,000 of 5,000 varieties was envisaged in 1964, and in a recent article received from India, I see there has been further development of the Zakir Rose Garden with more fountains. Every year a Rose Festival is held at the beginning of March, when flowering is at its peak. This is obviously a pleasure garden, but it is also

'Maréchal Niel', the Victorian rose still flourishing in India

important for breeding experiments, trials and assessment of roses for export and also the rose oil for which India was once famed.

The scented roses reminded me of Nur Jehan's discovery, taking me back to the times when first rose gardens were established in Kashmir and to the last century when roses from Europe became established in very different conditions. I wondered whether I might find any of them in this garden. I wandered over a little bridge to another part to see, some distance away, soft yellow spread over framework and felt rather like Robert Fortune in China. When I got nearer, there was no mistaking the inclined heads amid dark, glossy foliage. I sat in the shade of 'Maréchal Niel', smiling over my good fortune to have found the rose universally mentioned by many since its introduction in 1864, acclaimed alike by Dean Hole and Dr Pal, and feeling how fitting was this finale to my pursuit of roses in India.

However, I am still kept in touch with them through Mr J. P. Agarwal, Editor of *Rose World*, published by the United Provinces Rose Society in Lucknow, a journal reporting conferences, reprinting articles, reviewing books and providing up to date information on all aspects of rose growing, not only in India, but throughout the world. I am indebted to him for his help through correspondence and useful information, as I know he is much occupied in organizing a National Rose Convention, to be held in Lucknow in January 1989, when leading rosarians from other countries will see some of India's roses at their best.

Dr Pal kindly sent me the souvenir booklet published on the occasion of the Silver Jubilee of the Rose Society of India in 1984, in which I was very pleased to find the quotation on page 113. He tells me that the Mahatma frequently used this allusion to the rose, when emphasizing that quiet, unostentatious work was more meritorious than showy demonstration. This was an echo of the assessment of Joseph Pemberton and is an apt opener for this section – one to be pervaded by perfume from Hybrid Musks, attar and revived old roses.

CHAPTER 15

Revival in England

My first recollection of an old rose is of one with blue-green leaves and full-petalled pale pink flowers growing near the window of our nursery in Suffolk. Now, some sixty years on, I realize that it was an Alba and, although I well remember the blooms were not as large as 'Great Maiden's Blush', it could have been the smaller variety discovered as a sport at the end of the eighteenth century. A time of boarding school and working in London brought no thought of roses and I suspect, had I been challenged, I would have quoted the prevalent newcomers of the early twentieth century, Hybrid Teas, as representative of the genus. Then came the

war and in the Royal Air Force we met someone who advised, one dismal day, to look beyond the present ... have an aim ... why not think about growing old roses? My curiosity led to learning more about his collection in Gloucestershire and promising to go and see him there once the war was over. In late June, one blissfully peaceful day, we found them in abandoned luxuriance, many free-growing in an old orchard, and for the first time I realized that there was a simple and satisfying way to grow roses. However, continuous postings were not helpful in establishing a garden, although one or two bushes of old roses may still flower around married quarters, and it was not until I came alone to Hampshire in 1968 that I could begin to make the garden of roses I had first thought about twenty-five years before.

I knew nothing: books had to be bought, people seen and gardens visited. At Chelsea Flower Show – a good place for secondhand bookstalls – I found a copy of Edward Bunyard's *Old Garden Roses* (London, 1936), one certain to whet any rose appetite, with lovely illustrations, a wealth of historical background and excellent descriptions of roses up to 1840. It has been summed up by Graham Thomas as the first book for a hundred years which 'owed its inception to a deep-seated love for all the old roses'. The original may not be found readily today, but this is one of the American reprints mentioned in Part I and I advise anyone wanting to learn more of rose history in Greece, Rome, Persia, the Middle Ages, Italian Renaissance, Holland, France, England and China to absorb this scholarly account with contemporary illustration. Yet this is a book not only for aesthetes and academics but also for practical gardeners, as the second part gives some of the best guidance on recognition of the various classes to be found anywhere and, although the monochrome photographs are of cut roses, they clearly show the main distinctive characteristics. In his Introduction, Bunyard stresses points to be appreciated in old roses: their compact form and 'proportion of flower size to leaf size and to the bush or tree as a whole', compared with modern large blooms apt to destroy the balance of the plant. Their colour and fragrance are beautifully assessed: crimson Gallicas are 'rich without harshness', soft pink Albas 'delicate without feebleness', while 'for us in England summer or autumn would not have truly been if the scent of roses had not crossed our path'.

In the early 1950s, after a period of deprivation with little time for romantic concepts and when garden help was not as easily come by as in pre-Second World War days, there was an incentive to create beautiful, undemanding gardens and for these roses had to be treated individually rather than in anonymous regimentation. At this time a gardening column started to appear each Sunday in *The Observer* and over a period of fifteen years, Vita Sackville-West contributed her articles, many on old roses. Her own appreciation personalized them in detail: foibles were assessed, bad habits condemned, complexions described and charms praised, so that one felt almost compelled to make their acquaintance. Some of the articles were published in book form later, but now a new illustrated anthology has been assembled by Robin Lane-Fox in *V. Sackville West. The Illustrated Garden Book* (London, 1986). She writes from experience at Sissinghurst in Kent, where she created one of the first great modern gardens of roses and, although there is formal lay-out, they are allowed certain freedom; some are placed on the perimeter of beds to bestow fragrance near pathways and others billow behind as colourful backcloth. Further rose pictures will be found in this famous garden; like the immense pale parasol provided by *R. mulligani* (hitherto known as *R. longicuspis*) in the White Garden and 'Madame Plantier' pouring creamy blossom over apple trees. Vita Sackville-West appreciated how Edward Bunyard's book had revived an interest in old roses since the 1930s and realized it was about to be furthered by Graham Thomas. In her Foreword to his *The Old Shrub Roses* (1955), she praised 'a uniquely authoritative book', adding her own artistic assessment in likening their blooms to colours woven in Persian carpets or flushed on ripening fruits. Through her writing we appreciate the romance in roses, find poetry in their petals.

Constance Spry was another enthusiast, collecting and growing all she could find as well as demonstrating their decorative qualities to countless followers throughout the world and encouraging everyone with a garden to plant them. She, too was a devotee of both Edward Bunyard and Graham Thomas, quoting them respectively in her books, *Flowers in House and Garden* (London, 1937) and *Favourite Flowers* (London, 1959). In the earlier month-by-month survey, June is redolent with old roses and they are fully and appealingly described in two chapters of the second work. She found striped roses, particularly the Gallica, 'Camaieux', hard to resist and Mosses delighted her with their unique embellished buds and fragrant flowers, the old pink 'Common Moss' being her favourite. For long she had cherished 'Maréchal Niel' for a soft yellowness, but it would seem she loved best the deep crimson and purple roses – like 'Prince Camille de Rohan', dusky offspring of 'Général Jacqueminot' and 'Géant des Batailles' – and would carefully pour their blooms from elegant containers.

After our return from New Zealand I discovered that Graham Thomas had established his entire collection of roses at Sunningdale Nurseries, not far away from where we then lived. I first saw these in autumn when graceful *R. moyesii* stems dangled hips delightfully, golden leaves of *R. rugosa* glowed and *R. virginiana*'s had burst into flame. This was a very different picture from the one I had treasured from Gloucestershire in June and another to keep in mind until such time as I could start on my own garden. At Sunningdale I found Graham Thomas's concise booklet, *The Manual of Shrub Roses* (1956) describing every kind, from wild species through all the old varieties to Hybrid Musks, Modern Hybrid Shrub Roses, Climbers and Ramblers, giving details of pruning and general cultivation. Of the oldest he says in the Introduction that he is seeking 'to bring forth these lovely things from retirement'. I like that; he will not let them admit dismissal, but suggest they had graciously given way to allow display by modern competitors before being persuaded again to demonstrate their particular qualities. My well-worn copy of this little book, surely one unsurpassed in encapsulating so much rose advise in such slim form has, of course, been augmented by the famous Thomas trilogy: *The Old Shrub Roses* (1955) covering Gallica to Bourbon, followed by *Shrub Roses of Today* (1962) and *Climbing Roses Old and New* (1965) all three with later revised editions, the latter two enhanced by the author's lovely exact drawings and paintings. These encyclopaedic works came at the time they were urgently needed; here was everything to be learned about roses, as well as information on how to make beautiful gardens of them. I believe, without them, I would

have got nowhere. There is a particularly good section covering display of Climbers and Ramblers in the third, followed by comprehensive lists of those suitable for various positions and purposes (pp. 169–86). All three books contain references to well-known illustrations of various roses with expert assessment of quality; admirable assistance for a reader seeking accurate depiction.

Graham Thomas is also Gardens Consultant for The National Trust and he laid out their Rose Garden in the old walled kitchen garden of Mottisfont Abbey, near Romsey in Hampshire in the early 1970s to display one of the most comprehensive collections in England today and containing many rare older varieties. Of them he says, 'Together they form a group of plants with a colouring, style and fragrance that has never been surpassed and it is for these qualities, even more than their historic interest, that the National Trust has chosen to preserve them.' On arrival, every visitor should make sure of collecting the plan and list from the kiosk to help with identification because this is an ideal place in which to consider a nucleus for a garden of old roses and plants to grow sympathetically with them. The majority of each class is planted together; for example the Hybrid Rugosas are in the bed on the right near the entrance and a splendid collection of Hybrid Perpetuals in two long borders along the far side. The walls are clothed with Climbers, and Ramblers are decoratively grown over archways and up pillars.

I have already mentioned some of Mottisfont's roses in other chapters and so will now add just a few more I always find rewarding. Floriferous bushes of 'Leda' or 'Painted Damask' exemplify an unusually compact Damask; 'Mutabilis' of spectacular shades is outstanding among a brilliant collection of China Hybrids integrated with dianthus; and Bourbon 'Variegata de Bologna' festoons an old apple tree, its cupped blooms looking like striped candied fruit in a Hansel and Gretel garden. Harlequin Hybrid Perpetuals 'Baron Girod de l'Ain' and 'Roger Lambelin' are the better bent to show their unusual markings, 'Goldfinch', a well-named Rambler, has settled happily on a pillar and 'Constance Spry', one of David Austin's new English Roses with the old-fashioned look, spreads prolific pink blooms over the central part of the west wall. I am not yet entirely *au fait* with the new section, but as well as the romantic arrangement of Ramblers already referred to, I have discovered a single bright pink Moss called 'Goethe' and am impressed by a dense display of ground covering roses. However, I was delighted to be welcomed near the entrance from the original garden by another English Rose: a rich golden yellow in Centifolia form and, named 'Graham Thomas', it seems an admirable choice to acclaim a great gardener who has done so much to reinstate the old roses.

This rose is an excellent example of the important work of David Austin at Albrighton, near Wolverhampton, where he has a large collection of old ones as well. Over the last twenty years he has been amalgamating their charms with the qualities of the moderns to achieve short-growing shrub roses of graceful habit. We find, with his English Roses, the colour of 'Charles de Mills' in 'William Shakespeare', form of 'Fantin-Latour' in 'Heritage' and Damask fragrance in 'Mary Rose'. My only slight reservation with a few varieties is the heaviness of blooms on small bushes; but I have heard these roses praised the world over, particularly for their long flowering period. They are well

LEFT
English Rose,
'Graham Thomas', here
in The National Trust
Rose Garden at
Mottisfont Abbey,
honours the designer.

A delightful association of pink 'Debutante' and one of the darkest violet Ramblers, 'Bleu Magenta', Mottisfont.

illustrated in David Austin's *Handbook of Roses* and a second catalogue lists an admirable collection of hardy plants for rose association.

A rose garden within an even greater walled area than at Mottisfont will be found at Castle Howard, near York, where Jim Russell, who had also been associated with Sunningdale nursery, has amassed a comprehensive collection. This was originally conceived as a tribute to the memory of Lady Cecilia Howard and was completed in 1978. I particularly like the method used to display some of the larger old roses with the use of trellis; rectangles have been built out from walls – the better to circulate air, I imagined, but learned that this was not the object – and certainly rather lax Bourbons and Damasks do make more impact shown thus than when flatly fastened. Pyramids of bloom are also achieved with trellis and I recollect 'Blairi No. 2' and 'Gloire de Dijon' well displayed in this way, while more bouffant roses are contained in box forms. Wide borders of old roses, including a particularly lovely one of Albas, are well planted with foliage plants and succeeding flowerers – phlox, for example. I often quote a rewarding association of dark purple Bourbon 'Gipsy Boy', with silvery-pink Hybrid Musk 'Felicia' backed by *Pyrus salicifolia* '*Pendula*' and many such imaginative amalgams will be found.

Near the car park there is a splendid example of a Rugosa hedge with 'Fru Dagmar Hastrup' first spreading an abundance of pale pink flowers and later crimson hips, while on the way down to the rose garden there are fine free-standing roses in grass. A large glade in Ray Wood is devoted to species and wilder-looking hybrids, where a mass of flower will be found in early July, including *R. macrantha* 'Daisy Hill' and *R. polliniana* contriving pink carpets below, with an uncommon *R. soulieana* seedling, 'Wickwar' weaving white clusters through the trees above. Autumn brings a very satisfying medley of hips, with *R. wichuraiana* flowering at ground level.

I have been scanning a list of over 600 roses at Castle Howard in 1984 – and there will be more now – to find that they have come from as far afield as Bermuda, China, Denmark, France, East and West Germany, Switzerland, the USA as well as from Kew and other sources in Britain. I know well that there will have been reciprocation (I have had some lovely Teas, including a resilient 'Madame Wagram' from Jim Russell). This lovely garden in York-shire well represents current exchange of old roses around the world. Many private gardens are now growing roses informally, integrating old varieties with plants and shrubs and using species for wilder parts, but here I am going to describe two I know to be well favoured by the overseas visitors I direct to them. They are primarily geared to roses, but are entirely different in concept and are at Lime Kiln, Claydon, near Ipswich in Suffolk and at Fairfield House, in Hambledon, Hampshire.

Humphrey Brooke acquired the first from his father-in-law in 1954, 'a lovely wilderness', he says, and in subsequent years he has developed it into a rose garden founded on his own theories: no fertilizers or sprays allowed, but a surprising number of weeds tolerated; roses never to be cut back or pruned, but dead wood and flowers relentlessly removed. In this chalky soil they are allowed to develop into bushes of unusual proportion: for example, 'Perle d'Or' and 'Lavender Lassie' have trebled their listed heights and the remarkable diameter of 'Climbing Souvenir de la Malmaison' spans 20 ft (6 m). Whenever I am taken around this garden, I am reminded of Herrick, 'A sweet disorder in the dress, kindles in clothes a wantonness', because here the roses display an alluring appeal often disciplined out of the average garden and a certain coquetry is evident among those at Lime Kiln.

A rose planted there in the 1920s as 'Dresden China' by the Countess Sophie Benckendorf was rediscovered and renamed by Humphrey Brooke and now, as 'Sophie's Perpetual', she has been known to maintain her deep pink charms for him throughout the year. Near the house, tender Teas in pots flaunt their lovely flowers, while Hybrid Musks spread their fragrance in luxuriant abandon. In sheltered sunny spots, lax Bourbons dally pink cupped blooms with rosemary and potentilla or show them off advantageously in front of dark yew. Hybrid Perpetuals, a Brooke speciality, secreted in a small inner walled garden, allow their strong stems to be tumbled by beautiful blooms caressing campanula and cranesbill below. By the gate, _R. californica plena_, 21 ft (6·3 m) in diameter, stands as substantial sentinel, 'Paul's Himalayan Musk' pours fragrant cascades from trees and, most astonishing of all, 'Freia', who arrived by chance as a pink _R. moyesii_ seedling, holds court down in the old chalk quarry, dominating with dimensions of over 50 ft × 30 ft (15 m × 9 m) from thirty-seven trunks.

I was recently at Lime Kiln on a still golden October afternoon and we strolled round noting a diversity of rose fruits: like clusters of tiny orange grapes on _R. filipes_ roofing the garage, as veritable small tomatoes embellishing _R. rugosa_ and as plump blackcurrants on _R. pimpinellifolia_. Diminutive orange pears fell from _R._ 'Doncasterii' and a myriad of tiny flagons turned 'Freia' into a russet backcloth for this autumnal tableau. Over tea we acclaimed the final rose bonus and exchanged experiences abroad. Humphrey Brooke is well acquainted with the famous Rosarium at Sangerhausen in East Germany, of which he gave an interesting account in _The Rose Annual_ (1975), and this has been the source of many Victorian roses now liberated at Lime Kiln. I know he is among those most appreciative of the qualities provided by these nine-teenth-century beauties, so well displayed in this garden of magical growth and capricious charm.

In complete contrast, the garden surrounding Fairfield House of elegant

Early stages of training roses on trellis forms at Castle Howard. (2)

Regency architecture in Hambledon, Hampshire's village of cricket fame, is an example of careful choice and arrangement of roses by Peter Wake. He has cajoled them to advantageous display, either alone or with appropriate complementary neighbours, providing example for those wanting to find out more about integrating revived roses into gardens of today. Detailed plans are available for visitors: one covering Shrub and Bush Roses, the other listing Climbers – some 200 in all – and these provide clear guidance around the garden as well as ready means of identifying the roses. I am selecting aspects I consider particularly impressive and first place must go to an extensive display in grass, where large bushes are given freedom of growth but are supported inconspicuously by green stakes and cord – by far the best method of discreet control I have ever seen. Here are *R. hugonis* and *R.* 'Cantabrigiensis' to show the first yellow flowers of spring, followed by pinks of *R. californica* 'Plena', *R. forrestiana* and *R. villosa duplex* ('Wolley Dod') and, later still, *R. soulieana*, pale yellow amid grey-green foliage. With these are representatives of older varieties: Alba 'Celeste', Damask 'Ispahan' and 'Madame Plantier' as well as more modern 'Frühlingsgold', 'Marguerite Hilling' and 'Cerise Bouquet'. Walls surrounding three sides of this area are covered with Ramblers and Climbers and two I first saw here were 'La Mortola', the *R. brunonii* selected form, and 'Frances E. Lester', well scented from Hybrid Musk derivation. The fourth side slopes down to the swimming pool, where I always think the single bright pink Hybrid Musk 'Vanity' and cerise 'Rosemary Rose' were admirably selected for a vibrant picture with subdued red brickwork, whereas in contrast, 'François Juranville' and 'The Garland' cover a restful, shady arbour nearby.

In a smaller walled part on the east side of the house, 'Golden Wings', with allium and iris below, dominates a yellow and blue border and 'Graham Thomas' contributes an outstanding autumn display. Opposite, a massive 'Charles de Mills', the very flat-bloomed deep red Gallica, consorts with 'Buff Beauty', the one a good foil for the other and 'Roseraie de l'Häy', a Rugosa of wonderful scent, is backed by *Buddleia alternifolia* to produce a lovely liaison of purplish-crimson and lavender-blue flowers. At the far end, Moss 'William Lobb', climbs surprisingly high in *Genista aetnensis*, where the dark purple blooms are slightly muted by a mist of fine foliage. Deep red climbers 'Souvenir de Claudius Denoyel' and 'Ena Harkness' against white pillars make a dramatic approach to the front door, but on the south-west side of the house, paler roses of smaller scale have been selected for compatibility with delicate ironwork: climbing forms of 'Cécile Brunner' and 'Pompon de Paris' to crown a blue-grey canopy. Below, 'The Fairy' tumbles small pink clustered blooms on neat grey *Hebe pinguifolia* 'Pagei' in perfect scale and, to complete the quiet scene, the terrace beds are filled with soft pink and white roses, including 'Iceberg', 'Little White Pet' and 'Dame Prudence', well associated with lavender and silver foliage plants. I hope that this brief selection will give some idea of Peter Wake's thoughtful composition in the creation of his enticing garden, one well demonstrating the twentieth-century use of roses from many periods.

Finally – and importantly – we have in England a nurseryman with probably the largest collection of old and species roses in the world. In 1985, Peter Beales brought out his *Classic Roses*, a weighty, expensive book but

ABOVE RIGHT
A profusion of roses around Lime Kiln, Humphrey Brooke's Suffolk home.

RIGHT
R. villosa duplex **('Wolley-Dod's Rose'), one of many large roses well displayed in grass at Fairfield House, Hampshire.**

within two years already into its third edition, sure evidence of growing interest in the subject, especially in the USA. It is the first here to be profusely illustrated throughout in colour and covers both history and practical aspects of growing, with a valuable encyclopaedic account of over 1000 roses, to which I have often referred for this book.

I first met Peter in early days when he grew roses at Swardeston in Norfolk, finding him always ready with advice and, like Pemberton, gaining pleasure in just talking about roses. Then came the move to Attleborough, north of Thetford in the same county, where his present nursery covers 15 acres (6 hectares), with an extensive display garden included. More of Beales Roses may be seen at Mannington Hall Gardens, eighteen miles north of Norwich; and a three-day Rose Festival is held there at the end of June. Peter himself has bred some successful roses, among them 'Sadlers Wells', 'James Mason' and 'Anna Pavlova', a highly scented soft pink which in 1986 won a silver medal at the Genoa Rose Trials in Italy. As I have seen on my travels, Beales Roses are known the world over and, as already mentioned, Peter is an able rose ambassador in furthering co-operation with Heritage Rose Groups abroad. I have recently heard that Indian rosarians are delighted he is to be with them for their National Rose Convention to be held in Lucknow in 1989.

I am glad to be able to say that Lieutenant-Colonel K. J. Grapes, Secretary of the Royal National Rose Society, has told me that the formation of their own Heritage Rose Group is now contemplated. Organization of this is soon to commence and he is confident of success. Certainly, from the demand for lectures I am asked to give to interested horticultural societies and schools of garden design on the history of old roses and their place in gardens today, I am sure there will be wide support.

Part VI

MAKING GARDENS OF ROSES

I like my old roses mixed with other plants, rather than arrayed in beds by themselves ... I suggest a generous blend of flowers and foliage, to create a 'cottage garden' mixture, to give colour and interest from April to October.

GRAHAM STUART THOMAS, *The Old Shrub Roses* (1955)

R. 'Cantabrigiensis'

CHAPTER 16

Care and Arrangement

WHEN starting to make a garden of roses from scratch, there should be three prime considerations: how they are to be arranged, what is to be planted with them and, applying to both – a factor often overlooked – scale. It is important to remember that the flowers of roses can range from 1 in to 5 in (2·5–12·5 cm) in diameter and the height of bushes reach from 2 ft to 12 ft (60 cm–3·6 m). Diminutive flowers of 'De Meaux', for example, will be outdone by a neighbouring peony, while those of 'Nevada' will be competitive; or 'William Lobb' will stand aloof from a lowly viola, more suitable companion for 'Nuits de Young', a Moss of lesser stature.

One of the assets of the members of the genus *Rosa* is their diversity of habit; they may carpet the ground, billow in grass, scramble up or down banks, tumble over low walls, climb trees and cascade from them. These are roses for

Large flagon-shaped hips
of *R. moyesii*
'Geranium' hang in
spectacular autumn
display

the larger garden, as they are no respecters of limited space and it must also be borne in mind that although the majority of species roses flower early, they do have other assets and in their arrangement both early diverse foliage and later bright fruit must also be taken into account. They are ideal for the landscape, for wild walks and open spaces, whereas the average garden may require the application of a little restraint not only with them, but with many of both old and new roses grown as shrubs. Here the skill of arrangement is needed, but first a little guidance on planting, pruning and general care is necessary for the inexperienced.

Before placing an order it is necessary carefully to assess what space is available for roses. For instance, a rose of outstanding scent needs to be placed near a path or on a wall near a window, or if a certain colour scheme is envisaged, then it is best to mark it out carefully with sticks to judge distances between the roses. I have often heard of random choices from catalogues without relating them in any way to available space; most lists give dimensions, height followed by width, so an hour or two working out the best possible selection, is likely to save more spent on necessary rearrangement in a couple of years' time. Initial planting may appear scant, but spaces can always be attractively filled with annuals. It is best to place an order as early as possible to ensure that it may be met with the best plants available. If on opening the package rose roots have dried out, stand in a bucket of water for several hours before planting and if the proposed place is not ready, just heal in by cutting a trench, laying roots carefully, firming in and making absolutely sure that labels are not buried or damaged. If the new roses are to be grown where others have been for some time, it is necessary to change the soil – an exchange with some from the vegetable garden for instance – but assuming that the situation is new to them, it must nevertheless be well prepared: dug deeply, with topsoil kept for that position and a little well-rotted manure mixed in (although this alone should never be in direct contact with the roots). Should there be a drainage problem, I have always found a layer of dried bracken or heather in the base of the hole to be effective. The size dug out should be larger than the area to be covered by spread-out roots, about 18 in (45 cm) each way is usually enough and roots may need trimming, always leaving those with valuable little hairs – many gardeners in the past used to root-prune as a matter of course.

I mix peat and bonemeal in a proportion of three to one and sprinkle a covering in the hole, position the rose so that the union with stock is at least $1\frac{1}{2}$ in (3·75 cm) below ground level, because rain can wash away soil and leave the junction exposed, leading to suckering. If a rose needs support, the cane or post should be placed deeply in position before planting, thus avoiding root damage afterwards and then tied together securely, but not too tightly. When planting a climber near a wall, all roots should be fanned away from it. Having positioned the rose carefully, it is then topped up first with a good covering of the peat–bonemeal mixture, shaking the plant so it will filter between the roots, and firmed before finally the topsoil is replaced and trodden in. For follow-up treatment, I do very little for my old roses; they get a sprinkling of organic fertilizers in autumn (bone and hoof-and-horn meals) and, along with all the other roses, a liberal mulch of garden or mushroom compost in early spring, mixed with ash from my incinerator or wood-burning fire. Sometimes a little doctoring to supply trace elements lacking in the soil is a necessity. I use

become covered with a carpet of different greens and textures. Waterfalls of roses will cascade from the tall trees: 'Wedding Day', 'Bobbie James' and 'Rambling Rector', all frothing white blossom, reflected in the water and *R. palustris*, the American 'Swamp Rose' will be grown by the edge of the pond, adding a touch of pink to the otherwise cool white picture.

A compromise between the conventional and the wild was needed when friends added three quarters of an acre of an adjoining field to their garden. With a distant view of wooded hills and land sloping down to a little dell, I suggested walks on either side leading towards the country, these to be cut in rough grass and bordered with groups of roses – one would not make enough impact in an area of this scale. It was logical to carry on with an old-rose theme from a bed in the garden near the house and a trio of 'Cardinal de Richelieu' is now the first to be seen, this dark Gallica making a good focal point and leading to pink 'Conrad Ferdinand Meyer', the robust *R. rugosa* × 'Gloire de Dijon' hybrid, favoured by Rose Kingsley. Further down, *R. glauca* (one-time *R. rubrifolia*) makes a good foliage impact before a lighter colour scheme of whites and yellows is well displayed against the darker, distant background. 'Blanc Double de Coubert' is there, with lemon 'Agnes', another rewarding Rugosa, and one each of substantial *R.* 'Cantabrigiensis' and 'Frühlingsgold', while *R.* 'Paulii' rambles around the dell. The walk on the other side has a different concept in order to link up with an established orchard at the top, carrying on the fruiting theme through groupings of 'Penelope', 'Will Scarlet', 'Heather Muir' and 'Goldbusch' (the latter two being hybrids of *R. sericea* and *R. eglanteria* respectively), all producing a good show of hips. At the far end *R. virginiana* adds a brilliant autumn foliage display and now, six years on, the arrangement of the field walk with roses, ornamental trees and shrubs seems satisfactorily to have linked the original garden with the country beyond.

When thinking about roses to embellish an area dominated by swimming pool or tennis court, it must be remembered that these will probably be most used in the time of school holidays – July and August and therefore early summer-flowering roses should be avoided. I have recently thought out a rose plan for a new pool area situated in the corner of an old walled garden, where high weathered brickwork curves round. Obviously large blooms were needed here for impact. A deep red climber, perhaps two of 'Danse du Feu', always rewarding in late summer, placed in the middle might have pink 'New Dawn' and 'Madame Caroline Testout' either side and these in turn be flanked with white 'Swan Lake' and 'Long John Silver', a *R. setigera* hybrid and favourite of Humphrey Brooke. There is a narrow border in front of the walls and as planting there would be viewed from the pool, substantial impact was necessary. I suggested some Hybrid Musks and larger Victorian roses to be planted between and perhaps contrast – again for emphasis – with the climbers. 'Pax' and 'Prosperity', 'Reine des Violettes' and 'William Lobb', 'Felicia' and 'George Arends' with the reds, pinks and whites respectively. Across on the other long side of the pool in grass, 'Madame Isaac Pereire' of delicious scent, and 'Cerise Bouquet', both strong deep pinks could be allowed to grow freely and, for sheltered sunbathing, perhaps a screen of 'Sweet Briar', although past flowering, could add its fragrant foliage. I believe these selected roses, will be of the right scale and colours to furnish this pleasure ground.

Another commission is to design camouflage for a hard tennis court in a

LEFT
R. helenae cascades through *Prunus pisardii* in late July in compelling contrast.

147

be achieved by using roses of different heights and for a summer-flowering arrangement I would take the little Centifolia, pink 'Rose de Meaux' with darker 'Pompon de Bourgogne', backing them with moderate Gallicas, 'Tuscany Superb' and 'Georges Vibert', with perhaps Albas 'Amelia' and 'Félicité Parmentier' behind. This would produce a delightful display for midsummer, but if a longer-lasting one is wanted, then perhaps the China Hybrids are the most rewarding. A grouping could be made of 'Arethusa', 'Comtesse de Cayla', 'Irene Watts' and 'Madame Laurette Messimy' for a lovely medley of salmon, peach, apricot and orange shades.

Within the shelter of the house is the ideal place for growing Tea Roses and, in order to make the most of their lovely blooms, it is important to consider the background. If the wall is red brick, then white or pink roses are best; 'The Bride' or 'Rival de Paestum', for example. Conversely, the glowing tones of 'General Schablikine' and 'Archiduc Joseph' are better displayed against a white contrast. I think best of all with grey stone are the soft buff-yellow Teas like 'Madame de Watteville' and 'Safrano', perhaps in groups of three for a really good display and the latter responds well in a warm situation. It is almost essential to grow the climbing varieties in a sheltered position in Britain and certainly a patio planting of either shaded pink 'Adam' the first of the class (not listed as a climber, but lanky in growth), or white 'Devoniensis' in a large container would be worth consideration.

CHAPTER 17

Associated Planting

FROM time to time throughout this book I have mentioned pleasing associations of roses with other plants – a prime consideration when growing them informally as shrubs – and imaginative integration is imperative in order to create two scenes: one with roses predominating and the other to maintain interest when they have finished flowering. This is an entirely different concept from the garden rosebeds of one compelling colour of a few decades ago, although I appreciate that this is still necessary on a large scale for impact in public parks and gardens, when the odd rose among other planting would never be discerned. Some cities with rose-growing connections – Aberdeen, for example – have planted ribbons of brilliant colour on verges of approach roads and these roses cannot fail to provide an exhilarating welcome. However, this sort of planting demands attention, and today the average gardener with no help finds roses in mixed planting less bother and, moreover, can present other spectacles during their dormancy.

Flowers of the oldest roses are, on the whole, rather small and their often flat shape is not dominating: they can be overpowered by larger flowering

LEFT
'Madame Isaac Pereire', a Bourbon 'climbing' to 8 ft (2.5m) to waft delicious fragrance through windows.

neighbours like a buxom peony and their wonderful range of rich blue–reds be somewhat subdued by the brandish of a red-hot poker. Less obtrusive companions should be sought and small blue-flowered plants can provide the right, discreet accompaniment. Here, also, it is vital to have infillers standing by ready to bloom from August onwards, otherwise there will be colourless patches in the garden. Phlox, penstemon, fuchsia and hebe are all useful for the takeover and it is even possible to grow something like old-fashioned sweet peas through small rose bushes or a late-flowering clematis through the taller. Victorian roses, often larger and more dramatic, will prove competitive with most garden plants, but I do like to choose favourite nineteenth-century flowers (pink, pelargonium, sweet william, stock, campanula, delphinium or hollyhock) for their underplanting and as neighbours. These would have been widely used then for carpet bedding, and not with roses (except perhaps for a small edging to beds), but today they are decoratively used among them in groupings and not dotted about singly.

Chinas and Teas love the sun: I avoid detracting from their beautiful blooms by planting discreet associates rather than bold ones. For larger modern shrub roses, companions need to be of like stature: shrubs flowering between two flushes of bloom are ideal, or perhaps tall annuals to be tidied away and in their place bold ground cover allowed to run. Bulbs are a great standby too and informal groups of tulip will bridge many a gap; I like to plant red, pink and white with the older roses, and yellow around those of that shade, maintaining the same summer colour picture, while small bulbs and winter pansies can also be used in harmonious echo.

Foil is defined as something that sets off another by contrast and in this respect foliage is all important to provide distant backing or near accompaniment for roses. Two hundred years ago roses in wilderness planting had been shown advantageously among evergreens and Gertrude Jekyll stressed her appreciation of dark conifer background for them at the beginning of this century. However, the juxtaposition of a variety of shades other than dark greens had not been considered until comparatively recently and I shall consider how the lighter greens, as well as golds, silver-greys, glaucous-blues and deeper purples can all play their part in rose promotion. But if readers are about to flip over pages to see if ready plans are available, they will be disappointed. When I lecture on associated planting for roses, I always say I *suggest*, maybe *persuade*, but never *dictate*. I am sure that the intelligent gardener prefers to consider a suggestion as a base on which to develop his or her own ideas and I hope that this chapter will do just that: urge a rethink of a border, using some plants and shrubs already established or the creation of an island bed with due consideration of distant background or even the development of a wild garden. Of course, if I am asked to design from scratch a garden of roses with other plants, I submit plans for approval, but I see no necessity for providing them here, when generalizing on complementary and infilling aspects or specializing on maximum display of individual roses. However, there are helpful lists at the end of the book with information regarding habits and qualities of many roses particularly suited to the small garden.

As with the previous chapter on arrangement, I shall take different garden situations to demonstrate examples of choice of plants to complement and infill. I was once asked by a culinary expert whether it would be possible to integrate a few old roses into her small garden geared to herbs. This proved a most satisfying exercise; not only is the historical aspect correct, but also the soft foliage colours and small blue flowers of many herbs provide suitable foil and scale. An essential inclusion was *R. gallica officinalis*, the 'Apothecary's Rose' and 'Rosa Mundi', 'Président de Sèze', 'Belle Isis' (an unusual deep blush), were suggested as good examples of varied Gallica colour, all to be kept compact, clipped if necessary. For association with them, herbs of moderate size were selected: rue, hyssop, the true French tarragon, marjoram and basil, with clumps of chives and parsley. Behind them, 'Amelia' and 'Félicité Parmentier', moderate sized pale Albas, were planted with matt-leaved borage and sage and the contrasting light green foliage of lemon balm, bushing up to 2½ ft (75 cm), provided good foil for dark Moss, 'Nuits de Young'. At the back of this useful and beautiful assembly, to associate with the foliage of tall, bronze, feathery fennel, two delicate Centifolias were well displayed: 'Village Maid', softly striped pink on white and lovely 'Unique Blanche'. Various thymes were used as mats of ground-cover beneath the roses and to border this little garden, a low hedge alternating lavender, rosemary, and cerise 'Rose de Rescht', a remontant early hybrid. All the other roses were summer flowerers, but I was told that did not matter in the least – here herbs had priority.

Island beds are not everyone's idea of good garden design and have been condemned as bitty and vista disturbing. However, there are situations where a carefully balanced bed presenting all round viewing pays dividends and at Wisley some may be found to the right of the herbaceous borders leading up to Battleston Hill. Here, roses have been used with other plants in different colour schemes, the island beds in grass, and among them are groupings of yellow early summer shrub roses, purples and blues at midsummer and brilliant foliage and hips in autumn. For an arresting, isolated bed, perhaps backed by distant dark trees, fiery colours of orange and scarlet can be used – the hot ones I cannot have in my little garden of softly shaded roses. In the middle of a slightly irregular island there should be a spectacular rose, perhaps trained on an 8-ft (2·4-m) pillar and a long-flowering climbing Hybrid Tea, 'Reveil Dijonnais', derived from the Hybrid Perpetual 'Eugene Furst' in 1931, might be the answer here, stressing the theme with orange and red blooms. Two slightly shorter roses, one of ancient origin and the other a comparatively recent newcomer, could be included in the central planting: *R. foetida*

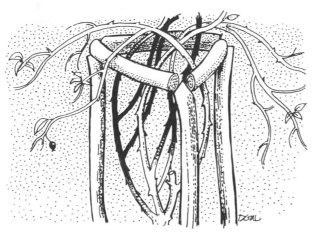

Construction of a tripod stand to contain a large rose; this can be camouflaged with suitable underplanting.

Border of summer roses showing discreet
companions: small long-flowering roses,
ground-covering plants and others to add taller
colour in late summer.

RIGHT 'Fantin-Latour', a sizeable Centifolia, falls
from tripod support to cool greens of fern, hosta and
alchemilla below.

'Bicolor', most spectacular of species and also known as 'Austrian Copper', has coppery-red single flowers reversing orange and sometimes bearing a few golden blooms of *R. foetida*, from which it sported four centuries ago. Another sport, discovered by Graham Thomas on the crimson Hybrid Musk 'Wilhelm' in 1947 and called 'Will Scarlet', will contribute a good second showing of that colour as well as orange-red hips.

Associated plants must echo and contrast: *Euphorbia griffithii* to add another touch of scarlet, *Potentilla* 'Tangerine' to flower long and two *Kniphofia*, 'Bee's Sunset' and 'Bressingham Torch' to supply poker-shaped shafts of colour. But the spectacle should not continue to disturb and I would add *Corylus maxima* 'Purpurea' to make a substantial background bush and shorter *Berberis wilsoniae*, their foliages of purple bronze and grey-green to calm, although the latter will later bring coral-berried brilliance. Around the perimeter of this bed, in groups of three, shorter roses will balance the taller: vivid China, 'Comtesse du Cayla', scarlet 'Korona' from Kordes thirty years ago, and orange 'Norwich Castle', a recent Beales rose. Around them *Papaver nudicaule* and *Eschscholzia* (poppies from Iceland and California) could spread and, again for a certain sobering effect at lower level, I would like some clumps of *Heuchera* 'Palace Purple' and *Iris foetidissima* with dark evergreen spears of foliage and later striking sheaths of orange fruit. This may be considered a somewhat extreme, hectic example, but it could provide the sort of exciting surprise enlightened eighteenth-century gardeners liked to spring on their guests.

I believe borders to be the best place to demonstrate the various qualities of roses; I love to plan them with other plants to complement and compensate, to see both filling gently curving contours, one colour leading to another, the whole integrated over all seasons. But this can be no easy, immediate achievement – mine are still not perfect after many years of trial. I think the best way to go about this sort of advice is to suggest segments dominated by various tones, from which different groupings can be selected to suit spaces available and plants *in situ*. Alternatively, an entirely new border could be made through use of one scheme enlarged from my initial lead. It must be remembered that too much dark colour should not be allowed to dominate a small garden, where its subtle occasional use can be most rewarding.

In the island bed just described, a touch of sober purple foliage was introduced for relief from intoxicating colour, but this shade can also be used to supply foil for pale roses, allowing them to illuminate the scene. For example the ivory of 'Moonlight' and amber of 'Buff Beauty' gain greater luminescence backed by *Cotinus coggygria* 'Royal Purple' and coral of 'Cornelia' is intensified against *Berberis thunbergii* 'Atropurpurea'. For such large Hybrid Musks, suitable underplanting is *Bergenia* 'Abendglut' ('Evening Glow'), to contribute broad burnished leaves in winter and pink flowers in spring. Shorter roses and their neighbours for this scheme could be 'Ballerina', Mrs Bentall's blessing for mid-border planting, its white-eyed lilac-pink clusters to be complemented by *Salvia officinalis* 'Purpurascens', 'White Wings', a superb single white Hybrid Tea with brown stamens, echoed by nearby tawny seedheads of *Sedum maxima* 'Atropurpurea', and 'Grüss an Aachen', a long-flowering floriferous cream rose, underplanted with contrasting dark *Viola labradorica* and infilling *Crocus tomasinianus* for winter footlights. If there is partial shade here, then there would be scope for *Helleborus orientalis* to contribute flowers of varied shades from cream to maroon in early spring. With them I would plant some Scotch Briars – 'Double White' and 'Old Yellow-Scotch', *pimpinellifolia* roses – to spread with runners and, with scattered seedling hellebore, an attractive wild-looking corner could be achieved, underplanted with primroses for the spring. Other suitable space fillers for this subtle border would be *Geranium sanguineum* 'Album' to form neat clumps and *Geranium* 'Johnson's Blue', taller, for a good splash of contrast around midsummer. Another useful infiller is *Allium tuberosum* bringing starry white flattened heads in autumn and always a good focal point in a dark assembly. As yet no bright roses have been mentioned for contrast, but there is none better than 'Rosemary Rose' brilliant cerise-red with possibly one of the darkest rose foliage and it could well be used with a light grey foliage plant to lead on to another grouping. Another good merger could be *R. glauca*, beloved by the flower arrangers for its unique foliage of grey green tinged purplish-pink and hints of copper. I also like its rich mahogany hips, adding warmth to an autumn day.

For glaucous association, I would restrict my roses to palest pinks with a few contrasting rich blue-reds, leaving strongest pinks for grey companions. Obviously Alba roses are complemented by their own glaucous foliage and this is itself the better offset by neighbouring darkest green, supplied by *Osmanthus delavayi* the year through, with a contribution of fragrant flowers, rather jasmine-like, in April. It is a slow-growing shrub, but worth the waiting and could be flanked by 'Céleste' and 'Great Maiden's Blush' with *Sedum* 'Autumn Joy' planted around their lower stems. This excellent glaucous plant, reticent in summer, will later infill with dusky bronze-pink flat flowerheads, to be embellished by butterflies. It is also a splendid foil for earlier display of dark Gallicas, 'Alain Blanchard' and 'La Belle Sultane', for example, both of unusually open form with prominent gold stamens. If there is enough space, 'Stanwell Perpetual' would be a good rose to use in this scheme, with lax grey–green foliage and blush blooms among the longest lasting in my garden – into the last week of November at the moment. It could be neighboured with *Caryopteris clandonensis* 'Kew Blue' for late summer association or by the pink stippled purplish foliage of *Berberis thunbergii* 'Rose Glow' as contrast.

Another long-flowering, but smaller blush rose, 'Fimbriata', is an unusual fringed Rugosa hybrid of upright habit and it might have as associates compact *Ruta graveolens* 'Jackman's Blue' of outstanding blue–green, and *Hebe carnosula*, a neat greyish-green variety. Underplanting should also be orderly: soft clumps of the blue grass, *Festuca amethystina*, low swirls of *Allium senescens* 'Glauca' and tussocks of purple-veined *Geranium renardii* among grey–green scalloped leaves. These would be suitable associates for three small bushes of 'Cécile Brunner', with no other rose to detract from the exquisite tiny shell-pink blooms, except maybe the even tinier 'Nozomi' of the same shade. I like to associate this prostrate rose with *Acaena anserinifolia* (*A. sanguisorbae*) of like habit and scale from New Zealand, letting them weave together a carpet of burnished green and pewter-blue foliage, where lilac crocuses might be scattered for spring infilling.

Pink roses and silver foliage seem to epitomize a summer celebration and, although rather obvious, this is the liaison I am asked most often to

implement; but it can be appealing, light and delicate, creating an almost fairy effect for the small garden. Therefore I suggest roses and plants of fairly restrained habit, the former all repeat flowering, omitting the larger shrub roses and their classic companions like *Pyrus salicifolia* 'Pendula' and *Crambe cordifolia*. If height is wanted a compact pillar could supply it. There are so many silver foliage plants of varied habit and form, I can mention here only a few. Quick consultation of a comprehensive catalogue – Beth Chatto's, for instance – will surely supply others for any rose situation. This scheme gives a chance to promote the typical rose-pinks of China, Bourbon and Portland, again with a touch of contrasting blue and I do not include anything heavy foliaged or dark coloured that would dampen an effervescent effect. 'Kathleen Harrop' is a moderate climbing Bourbon, eminently suitable for a pillar because, thornless, it will not be bothersome in training and could be grown with a clematis, perhaps *C. × jouiniana*, to infil with trusses of soft blue in early autumn. Two beautiful Bourbons, 'Reine Victoria' and 'Louise Odier' may tend to become leggy, but if their stems are swathed with *Artemisia canescens* and *Santolina neapolitana*, they will bend and blend their blooms into soft silver below. Portlands 'Comte de Chambord' and 'Jacques Cartier' make more substantial bushes and with them I like complementary billowing shapes of misty *Artemisia* 'Powis' and *Ballota pseudodictamnus* of matt-grey texture. Here, in mid-border, there could be a rewarding grouping of the classic Gertrude Jekyll association of 'Old Blush China' with lavender and another of rosemary and 'Hermosa', favourite rose of George V and planted in thousands at Sandringham. For infilling, I find *Nepeta nervosa* preferable to the unruly *N. gigantea* for a small garden; it makes little thickets of sturdy blue flower spikes from midsummer onwards. I also like *Anaphalis triplinervis* as a good ground coverer with soft grey foliage and clusters of white everlasting flowers on which in late summer 'The Fairy' will tumble pink blooms of the same size towards the border front. Here I would not spurn a little bedding out of the long-flowering miniature 'Perla de Montserrat', appropriately surrounded with tiny silver *Artemisia glacialis*, where *Iris reticulata* might supply early purple–blue – daringly, before the later pink and silver confection becomes established.

A border planting of golds and acid greens associated with roses may warrant a break with a path, as I have managed to arrange in my little garden, and this is just enough to lead the eye away from a quiet scene and down a yard (1 m) or two before returning to the other side for a different stimulating effect. This cool foliage proves ideal foil for the darkest roses. I well remember the first time I really appreciated the association: at Wisley I noticed an English Rose, 'The Knight' planted with *Ribes sanguineum* 'Brocklebankii'. This sort of colour scheme is becoming more and more popular and I will suggest a rather more imposing assembly here than previous examples and one which would possibly fill an isolated border. If there is room for a tree, then *Robinia pseudoacacia* 'Frisia' would make a good focal point as long as it is not too far away from the planting. As suitable border backing there are many imposing small trees and shrubs to choose from: *Philadelphus coronarius* 'Aureus', *Sambucus racemosa* 'Plumosa Aurea', *Berberis thunbergii* 'Aurea' are examples and even golden privet (*Ligustrum ovalifolium* 'Aureum') if never clipped but just thinned from the base, will contribute an elegant backcloth.

'Marbrée', a marbled pink Portland, well offset by silver foliage of *Artemisia ludoviciana*, kept trimmed below.

ABOVE LEFT
A border of Hybrid Musks, with plants of foliage interest to complement and infill between their flowerings.

LEFT
Low-growing 'Dunwich Rose' will break a hard edging or spread wide in partial shade of a wild garden.

Alchemilla mollis makes a suitably softening companion for the bold blooms of 'Ferdinand Pichard'.

Some compact conifers have bright golden foliage, but on the whole I am not in favour of their solidarity in this sort of rose planting; they are better used in a more open situation, as at the Royal National Rose Society Gardens of the Rose in England and at the Huber Nursery in Switzerland.

If these splendid associates are to be well displayed, then the roses grown with them must be under control and not allowed to sprawl; I would use Ramblers on pillars, with other roses given tripod support. It will not be a formal planting, nothing regular is contemplated, but it will be orderly, as befits a distinguished gathering. The pillars will be dressed with 'Rose-Marie Viaud' and 'Veilchenblau', rather pale purples, with 'Purity' and 'Sanders White' supplying restrained contrast. Hopefully, this quartet will flower between showings of 'Reine des Violettes', 'Souvenir du Docteur Jamain' and 'Général Jacqueminot'. Two tall dark Mosses, 'William Lobb' and 'Henri Martin' do not repeat, but they do continue flowering over quite a long period. The middle of this 10-ft (3-m) wide border is to be devoted to shorter dark roses offset by somewhat sculptural plants of acid yellow–greens: *Hosta fortunei* 'Albopicta', and 'Aureo-marginata', *Euphorbia robbiae* and *E. palustris*, while *Alchemilla mollis* will tumble lime green flowers on beautiful light green foliage in more abandon. Another softer aspect is provided by the golden form of feverfew, *Chrysanthemum parthenium*, its small white flowers linking with upstanding Hybrid Perpetual, 'Gloire Lyonnaise' behind. The other roses in this part of the border will be two repeating Mosses, 'Madame de la Roche Lambert' and 'Deuil de Paul Fontaine' and two long-flowering Chinas, 'Fabvier' and 'Gloire des Rosomanes'. Along the front Hybrid Perpetuals will be bent: 'Hugh Dickson', responding well to this treatment, 'Souvenir d'Alphonse Lavallée', one of the very darkest, rewarding on a lower level, and the crimson petals, piped with white, of 'Baron Girod de l'Ain', displaying to advantage. These deep blooms will fall on *Lamium maculatum* 'Aureum', its little violet flowers echoing the border theme and *Tolmeia menziesii* 'Variegata' of lime green foliage, both quick spreaders, with *Thymus citriodorus* 'Aureus' and *Oreganum vulgare* 'Aureum', golden herbs as flavoursome as their green counterparts. Along the front of this rather regal border, winter pansies could continue the theme of gold, purple and white and, around the hosta positions, clumps of deepest maroon tulips would bring interest to bare spaces.

Another aspect of associated planting – one to be encouraged – is an integration of species roses with flowers of the countryside. With today's emphasis on conservation there is incentive to devote part of a garden to growing wild flowers. These should not be collected from hedgerows, fields or woods. Seeds may be obtained from John Chambers, author of *Wild Flower Garden* (London, 1987) who has a comprehensive collection, including some species rarely seen in the wild (see Appendix for details). In a part of a field adjoining a garden, a few 'Sweet Briar' (*R. eglanteria*) could be planted as an informal, untrimmed hedge, providing shade for violets, while *R. canina*, *R. arvensis* and *R. villosa* (the old 'Apple Rose', bright pink with glaucous foliage) would make free-standing bushes near clumps of cowslips, ox-eye daisies and poppies planted to bring contrast and colour in the grass. Seeds of rare cornfield weeds – corncockle, cornflower and pheasant's eye – could be sown here and in damper meadows, attractive fritillaries, once established, would spread widely.

In woodland bordering a garden and benefitting from some sunshine, native roses of America, long grown elsewhere, will flourish in damp conditions. After the flowers of wood anemone, celandine, primrose, wood spurge and bluebell have faded, *R. nitida*, *R. virginiana* and lower-growing *R. foliolosa* will add pink blooms to a scene now enlivened with drifts of fireweed or rose-bay willow herb, a plant quick to colonize sites of old bonfires. They would be rekindled with the display of exceptionally brilliant foliage from these roses; fiery shades of red, orange and yellow, with a good show of hips, bringing warmth to the autumn woodland. From about 10 ft (3 m) in a tree above, *R. moschata*, the ancient climbing 'Musk Rose' will hang its beautifully scented white clusters from August to September and from another, honeysuckle could contribute its sweet fragrance earlier in the year.

A third wild scene with roses can be created in sandy soil near the coast, a natural habitat for Rugosas. When their flowers linger with scarlet hips and yellow foliage, I prefer 'Alba' to deep cerise 'Typica' and this lovely pure rose could be used to screen from the prevailing wind a garden where groups of tree lupin, yellow horned poppy and sea holly, adding a touch of blue, can be planted. Two other roses appreciate a maritime environment and would well integrate into this scene: prostrate 'Dunwich Rose' (*R. pimpinellifolia* 'Dunwichensis'), discovered not long ago on East Anglian cliffs, provides a carpet of palest yellow single blossom in early summer, followed by burnished foliage and fruit, and would spread around a glaucous sculpture of sea kale (*Crambe maritima*). The 'Burnet Rose' or 'Scotch Briar' (*R. pimpinellifolia*), known for some 400 years, grows best to 3 ft (1 m) in sandy soil and will contribute creamy-white, pink tinted single flowers and ebony hips to a garden of quiet colours within sound of the sea.

CHAPTER 18

A Ring of Roses

MAYBE the challenge, 'You'll never be able to turn that uninteresting little patch into a garden of roses' spurred me on to prove otherwise. When I came house-hunting in Hampshire in 1968, I found a small one exactly suited to my needs, but was disappointed by the garden. It lacked design; one third of it slashed straight across with man-made paving slabs, the rest a poor lawn surrounded by narrow straight borders, with a regimented rose bed in the middle and at the end, the only tree, a purple prunus, I disliked.

However, on reassessment, I found some points in its favour: the ground sloped gently to a good brick wall on the western side, solid fences on the other two virtually enclosed it and I appreciated a good vista of ornamental trees in neighbouring gardens ... there might be possibilities. Only very gradually, because I was then working full time in London, the idea took shape of a ring of roses encircling the lawn; borders were widened and curved to flow down from beds made in the paved area, now reduced by two-thirds. I certainly did not want a rose bed in the lawn, but I did want something to link up the two side beds; I extended the paving a little way into the lawn and excavated a small bed for prostrate roses so that the view to the bottom border, where the most spectacular were to be grown, might be uninterrupted.

I have kept records of rose arrivals over the last twenty years and see that the first order was placed at Sunningdale in 1969 for some large species to establish at the back of borders: *R. moyesii* 'Geranium', *R.* 'Cantabrigiensis' and *R. rugosa* 'Typica' – all now outstanding in stature. Then I needed a rose to embellish the prunus and, although the 'Paul's Himalayan Musk' I had ordered for its pale pink flowers turned out to be *R. helenae*, in the event, the latter could not have been bettered. The summer-flowering roses were hardly enterprising, but they were those I had often read about; I wanted each of the five classes to be represented by 'Rosa Mundi', 'Céleste', 'Madame Hardy', 'Fantin-Latour' and 'Henri Martin'. These formed the nucleus of the right, sunny border. 'Reine Victoria', 'Ferdinand Pichard' and 'Blanc Double de Coubert' went on the left and four Hybrid Musks in the bottom border, with 'New Dawn', for the wall, completing the order. There was one more early comer, brought to me by long-standing friends as a garden-warming present because they well remembered the *R. banksiae* 'Lutea' as one of my father's favourites on the wall of our Suffolk farmhouse. We planted it where the boiler in the kitchen warms the wall and there it has thrived through many a hard winter, invariably the first in the garden to flower. I see from my rose notebook that 20 April 1974 is the earliest record of the double yellow cherry-like bloom. These were my first eighteen roses.

The following year I decided to arrange prostrate varieties as ground cover. Rugosa hybrid 'Max Graf' settled suitably below the Hybrid Musks, and 'Raubritter' was pegged down firmly in the pool bed, but the third was a bad mistake – *never* plant *R. wichuraiana* in a small garden as, although it was a delight along the front of the right border for about three years, infilling with creamy flowers in August, it threatened a complete takeover and had to be extracted. Self-rooted bits were given to friends to cover stumps, low walls and banks in gardens of suitable dimension and the main plant was transferred to Suffolk, where it now covers an area of 24 ft × 12 ft (7·2 m × 3·6 m). Some scepticism was evoked by my idea of planting 'Raubritter' below ground level and Humphrey Brooke said that this rose, in his garden tumbling above ground, was never free from mildew – I was asking for trouble. However, with constant spraying, before the leaves break until they have fallen, I have kept that in check and this is one of the most successful of rose arrangements in the garden.

I had not yet decided what sorts to plant in the two beds near the house. However, the arrival of precious Teas from Teddington solved the problem for the one facing due south. Here I had, again mistakenly, planted three *Cupressocyparis × leylandii* to screen coal bunker and dustbin, but although they provided excellent backing for pale roses, these heavy conifers overbalanced the scene. On the replacement trellis, I put 'Mutabilis', the changing China I had noted ascending well on the Royal National Rose Society

'Raubritter' pegged in a sunk bed and 'Félicité
Perpétue' on the house, both flowering in July after
the old summer roses.

Initial stages of bending a rose; some Hybrid Perpetuals respond well to this manipulation.

headquarters at Chiswell Green. In 1970 I had called on Sir Cedric Morris, having been told of his inspired ideas for growing roses informally and, with understanding, patience and generosity, he told me a great deal as we toured his beautiful garden of irises, rare plants and random roses, all integrated through the eye of a skilled artist. I came away with slips of *R. nitida* and 'Rose d'Amour', kept in a bottle of water for a couple of weeks until I could put them in the shadier bed, an area for wild planting – the beginning of my collection of species from Scotland, Ireland and China.

Thus it was at the beginning: roses sparsely planted with few complementary neighbours, but through the 1970s, many additions came to these bare bones. By 1980 I could say 'not too bad'; the idea of a complete flow was consolidating, with no harsh colours to interrupt and the roses banked from the very low in front, through others ranging from 2 ft to 5 ft (60 cm–1·5 m) to the tallest behind, all complemented and infilled for each season. Recently there has been one major improvement: the badly laid slabs had always irritated me, little plants for the gaps never thrived although weeds did. The incentive to replace them eventually came through a last promise to a close friend and in memory of rose gardening together, well laid bricks curve around a half moon sunk bed containing 'Raubritter'. A description of my garden as it is today will show that it is possible in one some 75 ft (22·7 m) square, to tell the story of rose history and to demonstrate how most kinds may be appealingly displayed. This is endorsed by photographs for these last three chapters – all taken in it – and an explanation as we now tour round.

Starting off with the bed bordering brickwork on the right, 'Mutabilis', changing from the colours of chamois leather to pink to cerise, sparked off a colour scheme for that corner. Now the Tea–China bed has become a medley of them, plus a few clearer yellows. I was delighted to obtain a historic rose 'Parks's Yellow Tea-Scented China' from Peter Beales and put it on the trellis, although it has only flowered intermittently and two hard winters cut it back. It still sends forth strong deep red shoots, though, and I hope, covered through the cold, to coax more bloom. I have since planted 'Fortune's Yellow' there also and among these climbing Chinas, a Dutch honeysuckle associates most happily, entirely echoing the shades of 'Mutabilis'. Roses in the bed include Teas ranging from buff 'Safrano' to more acid 'Perle des Jardins' and blush 'Tipsy Imperial Concubine' through pinks to the fiery 'General Schlablikine'. 'Perle d'Or', 'Jenny Wren', 'Hermosa' (making an almost continuous display over five months) and 'Duke of York' are among the China Hybrids. The last, not well known, is worthwhile, being very floriferous with pink–white blooms on an open bush. 'La France', historic first Hybrid Tea, is here and, magnificent in the middle, the 'Moutan Rose' from China.

My Teas are minute compared with those I have seen growing in Auckland, Adelaide or San Marino and do not need the substantial companions I saw with them in gardens overseas. After various trials, I concluded that early flowering small irises, including 'Pacific Coast' varieties and later alliums were most suitable; they are also sun lovers, with strap and linear foliage providing just enough foil, and flowers in no way competing with the roses. Trouble-free alliums are under-used, or maybe unknown, but there is a great variety, ranging from tiny 6-in (15-cm) *A. insubricum*, hanging tiny rosy heads like harebells to *A. giganteum*, displaying large purple umbels 4 ft (1·2 m) high. The latter would be out of scale here, but besides those already mentioned, like swirling *A. glauca senescens* and late-flowering *A. tuberosum*, I would recommend *A. pulchellum*, both lilac and white, as lovely danglers, good in the garden and also dried indoors. Well-named foxtail lilies (pale yellow *Eremurus* species) bring another contrasting shape, displayed against shining foliage of *Choisya ternata* in a sheltered corner, thickly underplanted with snowdrops, and there are various clumps of spring, autumn and winter crocuses to flower among the dormant roses here.

Crimson of *R. moyesii*, now 10 ft (3 m) and the little China, lead on to the summer-flowering roses, Gallicas predominating, in the right border. They include 'Ohl', 'Boule de Nanteuil' and 'Belle de Crécy', all kept fairly restrained in limited space, although I do allow 'Rosa Mundi' free rein to hide bare stems of a straggly pink *R. moyesii*, grown from seed, as well as letting 'Common Moss' and the Damasks 'Madame Hardy' and 'Quatre Saisons' spread naturally. All the associated planting here either emphasizes the importance of reticent companions or prominent infillers. Self-sown aquilegias appear everywhere in many shades and I have also planted delightful *A. flabellata* of glaucous foliage and large blue–white flowers, seeds of which were most kindly sent from Ireland by a reader of one of my articles, who thought it right for my roses, as indeed it is, especially with 'Charles de Mills'. Love-in-the-mist also springs up surprisingly and, as blue is eminently right for these roses, towards the back of the border where 'Céleste' reaches 6 ft (1·8 m) or more, I have *Campanula lactiflora*, and *C. pyramidalis* with delightful *Thalictrum aquilegifolium*, arriving from I know not where, to contribute, like spun sugar, airy lilac heads. I have planted *Cyclamen neapolitanum* below *Magnolia stellata* in the middle of this border and flanked the lovely winter flowerer with two new pillar roses 'Blush Rambler' and 'Violette', replacing two lost ceanothus. Towards the front, again under control, I have infilling roses: 'Ballerina', 'Sophie's Perpetual', 'Yesterday' and 'Rose de Rescht', all repeat flowering and grown with clumps of shorter border geranium, *G. sanguineum*, *G. s.* 'Lancastriense' and *G. renardii*; all excellent front border plants, the first two flowering long. Standing by, in every space left in this border are many sedums, fuchsias, phloxes and penstemons, ready for their August display.

A typical Jekyll grouping of five 'Old Blush China' with lavender and backed by Portlands with rosemary fills the front of the bottom corner, where forget-me-nots sprinkle blue in late spring and have quickly to be tidied away before too many of their seeds establish a takeover next year. The bottom border is in full view of the house and is where I planted the Hybrid Musks. For long 'Buff Beauty' dominated the scene, beautifully lit by the setting sun behind, but a sudden sickening meant removal. Peter Beales thought it was due to the hard frost of two winters, but Jack Bentall said he had never known one so defeated. Nearby hebes also gave up; lovely *H.* 'Autumn Glory' and *H.* 'Great Orme', violet and pink, and so good for infilling between Hybrid Musk flowerings. Now I am reduced to hardy varieties, with insignificant white flowers, although I think their compact evergreen shapes, with the blue of rue and grey of *Cheiranthus* 'Bowles Blue', contribute to an element of contrasting rotundity here among spreading silvers. 'Cornelia' has made a well-formed bush, 'Wilhelm' is more straggly, but falls well on *Senecio greyii*, 'Prosperity' has replaced 'Buff Beauty' and the standard 'Felicia' from Havering-atte-Bower is planted in front of *Pyrus salicifolia* 'Pendula' – blatant emulation of the Castle Howard picture – although I have used *Geranium himalayense* 'Plenum' ('Birch Double'), one taller than most, with tiny violet–blue flowers and *Heuchera micrantha* 'Palace Purple' for contrasting association.

I have tried to echo the shades of both pear and prunus here, using silvers of various santolina and artemisia with purple sage and *Berberis thunbergii* 'Atropurpurea Nana' as companions for 'Madame Isaac Pereire', 'Honorine de Brabant', 'Marbrée' and 'Comte de Chambord', favourites among my Bourbons and Portlands. This is where blue hyacinths, originally grown indoors, bring winter colour. Along the front of the bottom border, a successful liaison of 'Max Graf' and *Stachys olympica* weaves a foliage carpet of glossy green and downy silver, attractive even without the pink roses. Now the border curves up to a point where it is suddenly diverted back down a little path and at this junction 'Stanwell Perpetual' falls on *Vinca minor*, as already described, with blues of geranium and tradescantia nearby. Between this assembly and the prunus, a sheet of bluebells surrounds *R. hugonis* after a random scattering of narcissi, with clumps of pulmonaria, crocosmia and *Iris sibirica* for a variety of flower and foliage.

The year through I am pleased by the different pictures supplied by *R. helenae* in the prunus. First to appear is one of tiny pink flowers on darkest twigs, next an association of young purple and green foliage, followed by heavy corymbs of white roses cascading down, as do the clusters of orange hips later and there is hardly a moment of void before the prunus flowers again. At one time this rose went up to more than 30 ft (10 m) in a neighbour's eucalyptus, until that too suffered in a severe winter; it now falls gracefully over the substantial stump on the other side of the mellow brick wall. 'New Dawn' covers a large area of this, 'Alister Stella Gray' is also doing well, particularly in autumn. I have recently planted the Boursault 'Amadis' here because this class was unrepresented in the garden and I like this climber's crumpled crimson blooms and later russet foliage.

The little path is illusory; it leads nowhere except to incinerator and compost, hidden by two bushes of my only rose creation. One autumn I was looking at *R. nitida*, thinking how dramatic it would be if those tiny leaves,

Autumn foliage of
'Corylus'; a new rose
from Bramshott.

LEFT Half-standard
Hybrid Musk, 'Felicia',
with complementary
planting. 'New Dawn'
and 'Alister Stella Gray'
are on the wall behind.

My mother, here holding roses in Edwardian days, later taught me about wild flowers; some grown in my garden today.

virginia creeper coloured, were larger. At the time those of *R. rugosa* 'Typica' were golden, deep-veined and bold, so I made a resolution next July to unite the two. I used *R. nitida* as the seed parent and *R. rugosa* for pollen and tied a piece of muslin over two flowers. One of the resultant hips fell off, but the second was noticeably larger than others on the bush. In October I buried it in a pot of sand, left this in the garden for six months and the following April rubbed out about twenty seeds. A year later thirteen had germinated, nine made strong growth in pots and by 1979 I could plant them in various positions in the garden. Flowers were medium pink and round hips a good red, the size of both midway between parents and the red-tinted autumn foliage good, especially on the plants in full sun. I was glad to be able to distribute these around to Peter Beales, Humphrey Brooke, Jim Russell and Peter Wake, then labelled just as 'N R'. I am gratified that it is now included in the Beales 1988 catalogue as 'Corylus'.

On the other side of the path, *R.* 'Cantabrigiensis' has developed into a beautifully shaped 10-foot (3-m) bush, a cloud of cream-yellow in late spring and later suitably coloured with *Clematis orientalis* twining through it. I have also planted *Pieris formosa forrestii* in front of the rose's bare stems; a reciprocal arrangement because the early tender red foliage of this shrub appreciates a little protection. Tucked away in this corner too, away from the old roses, *Euphorbia griffithii* brandishes fiery bracts. Although this border gets no full sun until late afternoon, it is an excellent situation for my darkest red roses, apt to burn with two much exposure at midday. This is where I use golds and pale greens as foil. 'Henri Martin', a tall, lanky Moss, spills deep crimson velvety blooms on *Spiraea japonica* 'Goldflame' and 'Reine des Violettes' mingles with a philadelphus. *Euphorbia polychroma* infills early with a mass of bright yellow bracts, before 'Prince Charles' and 'Cardinal de Richelieu' bring their almost maroon and rich purple shades above surrounding handsome foliage of *Alchemilla mollis* and *Astrantia maxima*. I put 'Blanc Double de Coubert' here for pallid contrast, with *Osmanthus delavayi* and *Sarcococca humilis*, dark evergreen shrubs to contribute fragrance in winter, and around them, returning to bright yellow, a splash of *Chrysanthemum parthenium* 'Aureum'.

For foreground spectacle, 'Ferdinand Pichard', bends low arches of cupped flowers, crimson-stippled blush, to fall on *Hosta fortunei* 'Albopicta' and lilac viola. The other Hybrid Perpetual, bent and fronting this border, is 'Souvenir d'Alphonse Lavallée', its deepest crimson–maroon flowers blending with those of *Lamium maculatum* 'Aureum' below. It was not my original plan to include the lovely Centifolia 'Fantin-Latour' on this side, but it became too large for the old rose collection opposite and had to be moved to more spacious surroundings. Now, nearing 8 ft (2·4 m), it reaches above the fence for sunlight and for a month delights with full pale pink blooms, some falling from a tripod support, camouflaged with fern, to the cool green below. This is a rose easily propagated from cuttings and, when tidying it in the autumn, I take some robust ripe wood which has flowered, about 8 in (20 cm) long, with a bud at each end and plant it in a mixture of sand and peat about halfway up the stem. These can be placed in a trench, well marked, or in a pot and should be rooted by the spring, when they may be left until planted out in autumn. I have found that hormone rooting powder makes little difference and have had less success using earlier wood still bearing leaves and covering the pots with polythene. Most Hybrid Perpetuals strike easily and this method of producing a small rooted rose in a pot makes a good present or donation to a fund-raising stall.

There is no problem of propagation with roses in the bed at the top of this border, where I grow small species and, in limited space, runners must be removed – thus my 'Dunwich Rose' has been widely dispersed. This bed is the antithesis of the sunny, orderly one opposite and, being the shadiest part of the garden, enabled me to make a woodland scene, although many of the plants are cultivars. Primroses and lily-of-the-valley grow under various forms of *R. pimpinellifolia*, with infilling trillium and hellebore around them. Ferns add a certain form: *Polystichum setiferum* 'Divirsilobum' making a swirling 3-ft (1-m) wide centrepiece, hart's tongue thrusting under the 'Rose d'Amour' and polypody surrounding *R. nitida*. *R. woodsii fendleri*, a fine upstanding species from America with lilac flowers and a good show of hips, connects this bed with the rest of the border. A pollarded *Acer negundo* 'Variegatum' presides over the assembly, providing dappled shade, with *R. davidii* growing among its lower branches. In early summer, 'Dunwich Rose' spills over the brickwork and in winter is infilled with violets. Also, carefully watched in the front of this bed are the treasured two seedlings from China; one prostrate, the other upright, yet to show their colours. Shrubs here may come as a surprise, but it is a fairly isolated corner where I could have a gaudy touch in spring and early summer from small Japanese azalea. In autumn their foliage, together with the metallic tints of these species roses, makes a spectacular display. The bed is never disturbed, there are too many precious root runners and little room for weeds, but every spring, it gets a liberal mulching of peat.

In the pool, 'Raubritter' holds masses of small pink cupped blooms for a month or more and makes no mess; there could be no better rose for such a situation. It readily roots where pegged to the ground and this method of layering is another easy one for propagation and distribution. In winter *Crocus tomasinianus* flowers through the bare stems, followed by a broad band of blue muscari round the perimeter and, before 'Raubritter' blooms, I place pots of the little Centifolia 'De Meaux' close by for colour interest while, afterwards, miniatures will maintain it well until the frosts. Around them I plant the tiniest viola and mignonette. With *R. banksiae* 'Lutea' and 'Madame Pierre Oger' on the south side of the house, 'Gloire de Dijon' flowers long and in July 'Félicité Perpétue' pours down from the north-west corner.

I used not to grow roses in my 'front', open to the road, until criticized for not indicating my whereabouts more obviously. There was little scope: small straight-edged beds by a pathway and a narrow border indicated formal planting while, with an aspect slightly south of east, white was the obvious choice for lighting the scene at the end of the day. I am grateful to Peter Beales for his suggestion of 'Horstmann's Rosenresli', a Floribunda of 1955 and new to me, as it has proved most rewarding: compact, fragrant, free-flowering, its full clusters tinged with a touch of green towards the centre on first opening. With careful cutting back, I get three flushes of bloom to last well into November. Six went along the little boundary border, underplanted with *Viola cornuta* 'Alba' and in beds either side of the front door I put trios of Polyantha, 'Yvonne Rabier' and Hybrid Perpetual 'Gloire Lyonnaise'. None of these roses needs support and all are eminently suitable for the conventional

'Sophie's Perpetual' has bestowed shaded pink blooms around the world: from Suffolk to Sangerhausen to South Australia.

approach to an ordinary, square little modern house with a neat, white row fronting them – pansy in winter, petunia in summer, my only concession to bedding out. However, there are no bare beds to be hoed and *Tiarella cordifolia* produces a foam of delicate creamy-white flowers in early summer and a dense carpet of fresh green foliage turning pink–bronze in winter. This colour is also contributed by the layered leaves of *Epimedium* × *versicolor* 'Sulphureum' in spring, clumped round stems of 'Boule de Neige', Bourbon trained on the house, and 'Madame Alfred Carrière', Noisette flowering on the garage wall over a long period. Now, for those coming to see my little garden for the first time, a directive, 'Look for the white roses' works well. Diverting the eye towards colour, another pink 'Raubritter', grown from a small rooted piece in the sunk bed, tumbles with purple *Geranium procurrens* to clothe the low wall by a side path leading to 'Mutabilis' on the trellis.

That is where the tour began and we have come full circle. When I make it on my own, I often think of another vast ring of roses extending around the world and, through those come to my garden from afar, I am reminded of the many kind people I have met and beautiful gardens I have seen in different countries. I also appreciate that making gardens of roses, however small, and savouring their qualities can provide therapy through contemplation and relaxation, an aspect of horticulture emphasized in China. Thus, busy lives of today may benefit, as others gained comfort from rose remedies of apothecaries long ago.

A ring of roses from my garden on July 4, representing various classes

1   'Céleste'
2   'Apothecary's Rose'
3   'Madame Hardy'
4   'Fantin Latour'
5   'Henri Martin'
6   'Mutabilis'
7   'Old Blush'
8   'Madame Isaac Pereire'
9   'Ferdinand Pichard'
10 'Félicité Perpétue'
11 Scots Briar 'Double Pink'
12 'General Schablikine'
13 *R. davidii*
14 *R. nitida*
15 'Buff Beauty'

APPENDIX I

The following lists have been compiled to help those wishing to make a small garden of roses. Careful selection will provide some interest from spring until late autumn with a variety of colour. Most of these roses have a good fragrance and none should prove too invasive.

1. Summer-flowering roses of compact habit

Camaieux (Gallica)	Soft crimson–purple, splashed white
Tuscany (Gallica)	darkest red
Alfred de Dalmas (Moss)	blush
La Belle Distinguée (*R. eglanteria* x)	rosy crimson
Félicité Parmentier (Alba)	palest pink, yellowish buds.
Leda or Painted Damask	blush tipped crimson

2. Summer-flowering roses, better with some support

William Lobb (Moss)	violet purple
Henri Martin (Moss)	deep crimson
Madame Hardy (Damask)	white
Céleste (Alba)	pale pink
Fantin-Latour (Centifolia)	pale pink
Tour de Malakoff (Centifolia)	cerise–violet–lavender

3. Repeat-Flowering roses of compact habit

Arthur de Sansal (Portland/Damask)	crimson
Jacques Cartier (Portland)	deep pink
Rose de Rescht (Portland)	deep cerise
Hermosa (China)	clear pink
Old Blush (China)	silvery pink
Cécile Brunner (Polyantha)	pale pink

4. Repeat-Flowering roses, better with support or training

Coupe d'Hébé (Bourbon)	pale pink
Madame Isaac Pereire (Bourbon)	deep cerise
Honorine de Brabant (Bourbon)	pale pink, splashed crimson–lilac
Baron Giron de l'Ain (Hybrid Perpetual)	crimson, tipped white
Hugh Dickson (Hybrid Perpetual)	dark red
Reine des Violettes (Hybrid Perpetual)	violet–lilac–purple

5. Ramblers and Climbers of moderate growth for walls or pillars

Blush Noisette	pale lilac pink, repeat flowering
Céline Forestier (Noisette)	pale yellow, repeat flowering
Goldfinch (Rambler)	gold–yellow
Amadis (Boursault)	purplish pink
Phyllis Bide (Rambler)	yellow–pink–cream, repeat-flowering
R. moschata (Musk Rose)	creamy white, late flowering

6. Tumbling and prostrate roses

The Fairy (Modern Shrub)	pale pink
Raubritter	clear pink
Scintillation (*R. macrantha* x)	blush
Snow Carpet (Miniature)	white
Max Graf (*R. rugosa* x)	bright pink–white centre
Nozomi (Miniature)	pale salmon pink

7. Roses for pots

Pompon de Bourgogne (Gallica)	purplish pink, small blooms
Rose de Meaux (Centifolia)	pink, small blooms
Irene Watts (China)	blush
Safrano (Tea)	buff yellow
General Schablikine (Tea)	coppery-red
The Reeve (English Rose)	dusky pink

8.   Recent repeat-flowering roses to associate with older varieties

Yesterday (Modern Shrub)	purplish pink
Ballerina (Modern Shrub)	lilac–pink, white eye
White Wings (Hybrid Tea)	single white
Cardinal Hume (Modern Shrub)	purple
Thisbe (Hybrid Musk)	buff yellow, good contrast
Roseraie de l'Haÿ (*Rugosa* ×)	crimson–purple

9.   Early-flowering species roses

R. dunwichensis	cream, low, spreading
R. pimpinellifolia 'Double White'	white, moderate, spreading
R. pendulina	purplish, neat bush
R. foetida 'Bicolor'	brilliant copper/orange, medium
R. hugonis	primrose-yellow, large bush
R. xanthina 'Canary Bird'	bright yellow, tall

10.   Roses for outstanding foliage, stems and hips

Penelope (Hybrid Musk)	burnished spring foliage, celadon–coral pear-shaped hips
R. webbiana	delicate ferny foliage, purplish stems, abundant scarlet bottle-shaped hips
R. glauca (formerly *R. rubrifolia*)	glaucous, tinted purple foliage and stems, oval mahogany hips
R. nitida	crimson autumn foliage, bristly copper-red stems, small red hips
R. virginiana	fiery-tinted autumn foliage, red–brown stems, round orange–red hips
Fru Dagmar Hastrup (*R. rugosa* ×)	bold gold autumn foliage, very large globular crimson hips

APPENDIX II
Addresses of organizations or people referred to in text

PART I

The Bermuda Rose Society
PO Box 162,
Paget, Bermuda

Heritage Roses
Miriam Wilkins,
925 Galvin Drive,
El Cerrito,
CA 94530, USA

Barbara Worl,
Sweetbrier Press,
536 Emerson St
Palo Alto, CA 94301, USA

Heritage Rose Foundation,
c/o Mr and Mrs John Butler
9700 Cattail Road,
Chesterfield,
VA23832, USA

PART II

Y. C. Shen,
420 Wildwood Drive,
South San Francisco,
CA94080, USA

Chen Yu Hua,
Bei Fang Rose Company,
7 Bai Shi Quao Road,
Beijing, China

PART III

Heritage Roses in Australia
Mr Pat Hart (Membership Secretary),
79 Atherton Street, Downer,
Aust. Capital Territory 2606, Australia

Heritage Roses New Zealand
Mrs Toni Sylvester,
37 Churchouse Road,
Greenhithe, Auckland, New Zealand

PART IV

Mr Göte Haglund,
Stationsvagen 6,
S–26044, Ingelstad, Sweden

Société Française des Roses
(also Les Amis des Roses)
Parc de la Tête d'Or,
69459 Lyon, Cedex 3, France

PART V
Peter Beales Roses,
London Road,
Attleborough,
Norfolk, NR17 1AY, England

Royal National Rose Society
Chiswell Green,
St Albans,
Herts, AL2 3NR, England

UP Rose Society
(J. P. Agarwal)
B/110 Mahanagar,
Lucknow, India

David Austin Roses
Bowling Green Lane,
Albrighton,
Wolverhampton WV7 3HB,
England

PART VI
John Chambers, Wild Flower Seeds,
15 Westleigh Road,
Barton Seagrave,
Kettering, Northants NN15 5AJ,
England

Beth Chatto,
Unusual Plants,
White Barn House,
Elmstead Market,
Colchester, Essex CO7 7DB, England

BIBLIOGRAPHY

Rather than using annotation, random references to books, periodicals and catalogues have been noted in the appropriate context and the following have been referred to generally.

Beales, Peter. *Classic Roses* (London, 1983)
Buist, Robert. *The Rose Manual*, facsimile of 1st ed. 1844 (New York, 1978)
Bunyard, Edward. *Old Garden Roses* (London, 1936)
Fletcher, H. L. V. *The Rose Anthology* (London, 1964)
Foster-Melliar, A. *The Book of the Rose* (London, 1905)
Griffiths, Trevor. *My World of Old Roses* (Christchurch, 1983)
Hadfield, Miles. *A History of British Gardening* (London, 1969)
Harkness, Jack. *Roses* (London, 1978)
   Makers of Heavenly Roses (London, 1985)
Henslow, T. G. W. *The Rose Encyclopaedia* (London, 1922)
Hibberd, Shirley. *The Rose Book* (London, 1864)
   The Amateur's Rose Book (London, 1894)
Reynolds Hole, S. *A Book About Roses* (London, 1869)
Jekyll, Gertrude, and Mawley, Edward. *Roses for English Gardens* (London, 1902)
Keays, Ethelyn Emery. *Old Roses*, facsimile of 1935 edition (New York, 1978)
Kingsley, Rose G. *Roses and Rose Growing* (London, 1908)
Miller, Philip. *The Gardeners Dictionary*, 8th ed. (London, 1768)
Nottle, Trevor. *Growing Old Fashioned Roses* (New South Wales, 1983)
Paul, William. *The Rose Garden*, 8th ed. (London, 1881)
Pemberton, J. H. *Roses, their History, Development & Cultivation* (London, 1908)
Polya, R. *Nineteenth Century Plant Nursery Catalogues of South-East Australia*, La
   Trobe University Library Publication no. 24, (Bundoora, 1981)
Rivers, Thomas. *The Rose-Amateur's Guide*, 11th ed. (London, 1877)
Ross, Deane. *Rose Growing for Pleasure* (Melbourne, 1985)
Sanders, T. W. *Roses and their Cultivation*, 7th ed. (London, 1911)
Shepherd, Roy E. *History of the Rose*, facsimile of 1954 ed. (New York, 1978)
Steen, Nancy. *The Charm of Old Roses* (Wellington, 1966)
Strabo, Walahfrid. *Hortulus*, 1510. No. 2 The Hunt Facsimile Series (Pittsburgh, 1966)
Thomas, Graham Stuart. *The Old Shrub Roses* (London, 1955)
   Manual of Shrub Roses (London, 1956)
   Shrub Roses of Today (London, 1962)
   Climbing Roses Old and New (London, 1965)
Young, Norman. *The Complete Rosarian* (London, 1971)

Note: Bold figures denote pictures. Some roses appear larger than actual size.